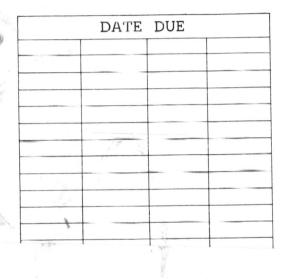

DATE DUE			

Mill Child

MILL
CHILD

Ruth Holland

Crowell-Collier Press

Collier-Macmillan Limited, London

Picture Credits

The Bettmann Archive, vi, 18, 31, 50, 58-59, 60-61, 78-79, 100, 123; Culver Pictures, Inc., ii-iii, 10 (a, b, c,), 45, 73, 91, 95, 115; Lewis W. Hine, George Eastman House Collection, 110; Historical Pictures Service—Chicago, 10 (d), 20, 21, 27, 38, 67, 83, 103; United Press International, 132-33.

Library of Congress Catalog Card Number: 75–92072
The Macmillan Company
866 Third Avenue
New York, New York 10022
Collier-Macmillan Canada Ltd., Toronto, Ontario
Printed in the United States of America

10 9 8 7 6 5 4 3 2

CONTENTS

*While there was still good light, everyone
who lived in the cottage worked*

Chapter One

IN THE COTTAGE

Once there was no clock in the house. The morning sun woke the chickens and the dog. The dog stretched and yelped and woke Mama. Then Mama knew it was time to get up. Morning time. Time to light the fire, start the porridge, set the bacon to frying. Time to haul water from the well, feed the chickens and the hog, milk the cow. Outside the little houses, dogs scratched at the doors, still yelping for their breakfasts. Pretty soon the children would be up yelping just as loudly for theirs.

In their warm beds, the children yawned and stretched and yawned again. Some pulled the covers over their heads. But it was no use. The sun and the sounds and the smells simply wouldn't go away. Day had come. It was morning time for sure. Soon Mama would be chasing after them to do their chores and Papa would be grumbling about the loom standing idle. They reached for their shirts and overalls or skirts hanging on pegs nearby. Then the clever, agile ones even managed to get dressed while still beneath the warm bed covers.

First the farm chores and then the spinning. That was the order of the day. While there was still good light, everyone worked. Old and young, girls and boys, mother and father, even grandparents—each had his own job to do. Anyone who was part of the family helped keep it going.

Only the land could not cooperate. Craggy, stony, inhospitable, the New England soil was just not fertile. The climate wasn't much help either. There were only four really warm months in which to raise a crop—and that on poor soil. Obviously, farming was no way to get rich, or even feed a family. No wonder New Englanders found other ways to support themselves.

When they first came to America, they had visions of endless acres of virgin land simply waiting for the plow. It all seemed too good to be true. And it was. Too good to be true. They managed to grow potatoes and fruit trees, corn and tomatoes, feed for the animals, but rarely more than that. Even in the good years, when summer seemed less restless to be off and away and the days were still long in September, even in those years there was not enough crop left over to sell.

In the South, farmers were doing just fine, growing rice, indigo, tobacco and, after a while, cotton. With much of the work done by Negro slaves, they were able to grow enough for their own use and a great deal more for export. Many years later, some of the children and grandchildren of those early New Englanders got to do what their parents had dreamed of. Out in the West, across Kansas, Iowa, Illinois and Montana, as far as the eye could see, farmers raised miles of yellow thistle-topped wheat. Enough to use and enough to store. Enough to sell and enough to get rich on.

But all that came later. After the pioneers and the covered wagons, the Gold Rush and the railroad, and after the New England farmers found another way to make a living. Oh, they kept their small farms, all right. To feed the family and the livestock and to have the pleasure of watching things grow. But to make money, they needed something else. They needed something to sell.

They took to making things, using the materials at hand and the skills they'd brought with them from the old country. Some cut down the forests and built many-masted sailing schooners that were as swift as any ships on the sea. Some built furniture, sturdy, simple, meant to last a lifetime and lasting longer.

The sea was as rich as the land was barren. Mackerel, salmon, cod seemed waiting to be caught. Young boys and their fathers went out in small boats that they'd built together. When they had a fine catch, they sold it. In England, Spain and Italy people needed the food. The fish was dried and smoked so it wouldn't spoil and sold to the master of one of those mighty sailing vessels.

They were grand ships, those early American schooners, as good as any the English could make. And the English were paid to make the best. But the American boys had learned at their fathers' knees. And their fathers had learned in England. Even a four-year-old was not too young to hold the hammer while his father used the saw. And each day, the boy was trusted to do more. Not only because his father wanted him to learn the trade, but because, in fact, fathers needed their children's help.

There was still another good common-sense reason for children's working alongside their parents. Here was a way of raising children so that their mothers and fathers could keep an eye on them. This way, a man could teach his sons more than a trade. A mother could teach her daughters more than how to sew and cook and keep house. As they worked together, parents could tell their children what they believed of the world and God, of good and evil. Parents could hope to keep their own moral codes alive in their children.

Where whole families worked at home, in their own cottages, the bonds were even stronger. From sunup, when Mama started the fire, stirred the porridge, roused the children for their chores, the family worked together.

The most successful of these New England "cottage industries" was the manufacture of cloth.

Just as it had been back in England, the work was divided roughly into two main categories. There was the work of spinning and the work of weaving. Women and children did the spinning. They carded the wool, combing and brushing out the tangles to make it ready for spinning. Then they spun it into thread and prepared it for the weaver.

The men wove. Weaving required considerable skill and so it was thought of as a "man's job," not quite suitable for the "limited abilities" of women and children. Some people bragged that they could look at a piece of cloth and know whose loom it had come from.

A good weaver was a proud man. He worked at an

important trade and he worked well. His loom was set up in the most comfortable part of the cottage, close to the fire in winter, near the open door to catch summer's breezes when the season changed. His wife and children often worked in half darkness to save their precious candles for him.

Still, if business fell off for a bit and there was less call for his cloth, it was not so much of a problem. After all, his cottage stood on his own land and the land needed him. There was plowing and planting to be done in the spring. In the fall, the fruit must be plucked from the trees, the vegetables harvested.

If the weaver couldn't afford to take time from his loom, he had to stretch the day.

First, he was a farmer, since chickens and pigs, a cow and a horse can't wait to be fed. Even seeds can't wait to be sown. But a loom can wait for its threads. Farm chores done, the weaver washed the soil from his hands and went from agriculture to industry.

It was hard work. The days were long and full. There wasn't much time for play in the spring and fall when the farm needed special tending. It was hard work for the weaver and it was hard work for the spinners, too. Because everyone who lived in the cottage worked at its industry.

Some weavers kept sheep and carded their own wool. An eight- or nine-year-old child could easily tend the sheep. Even younger children could help their mothers with the carding. They cleaned and combed and disentangled the curly fibers of wool to get them ready for spinning.

Older girls learned how to use their mothers' spinning

wheels. Using the carded wool, or cotton bought from southern planters, they stretched the fibers, pulling them out and twisting them into threads as long and fine as they could make.

Even a baby could hold a stick, or bobbin, while an older child wound the spun threads around it.

Now the threads were ready for the weaver. In large families, it seemed as though one of the boys was always at his father's side, pulling thread through the shuttlecock and learning how to guide it in and out across the loom. And sometimes, waiting impatiently just behind the oldest boy, was a younger brother eager for his turn to learn the family art. Eventually, men taught their wives and daughters, too. The finer the thread and the art of the weaver, the finer was the cloth he produced.

Rich, artistocratic American gentlemen, accustomed to sending to England or Europe for their fine broadcloth shirts, discovered soon enough that a little ways out of town, down a country lane, stood many a small cottage where one could buy cloth as good or better.

Inside, the cottage fairly burst with activity. If someone left the spinning wheel to stir the cooking kettle, another pair of hands took over. Children hummed and sang, played counting games, told stories, while their fingers flew through the curly wool. After a while, though, they were bound to get restless. Especially on sunny days. The cottages were small. And there they were, all together, under one roof. One of the older children or Mama would turn around and see that the little ones were bickering or fidgeting or simply being bored. Then off they'd be sent for a run in the woods and a good game of tag.

If one of the children seemed sick or just too tired to work one day, it was fun to rest at home in bed with all the busy family bustling about. It wasn't as though Mama went out to work. She was right there, right at home. She could leave her spinning wheel a while to cook up a nourishing broth. She could sit at the sick child's bedside a bit. Tell him a story. Sing him a song.

There was no clock in the house with long hands to rule their lives. There was no clock to tell them when to start work and how long to stay at it. The spinning wheel could always wait and so could the loom. No clock said the children may have just five minutes to eat their dinner, just one minute to play and no time off for daydreaming. No clock timed how long Mama spent at a sick child's bedside.

The little children working alongside their parents in cottage industries put in long, hard days. Whether they were making cloth, building boats, constructing furniture or forging metal, they were learning as they worked. Some days were harder than others, but the children could understand that. Perhaps there was a very big order to fill. Perhaps one merchant needed his order in a terrible hurry. Then they might have to work by candlelight way into the night. But, on another day, when they smelled spring in the air, they could run from the cottage and into the fields. Rolling on the meadow, they'd stretch their limbs and pull at the grass instead of that sticky old lamb's wool.

What needed to be done and what they needed to do— that was the children's clock. That was their clock and their boss and their overseer. Until, of course, Mr. Hargreaves came along.

Chapter Two

AT THE MILL

In Lancashire, England, a fast and skillful weaver named James Hargreaves patented an invention which signaled the beginning of the end of cottage industries.

As he waited for more thread for his loom, Hargreaves watched the spinners at their wheels. Why couldn't one person, pushing one wheel, turn several spindles at once? In that way, one person could spin several threads at one time.

This first spinning machine was nicknamed the spinning jenny, although she worked so fast her name ought to have been "jennies."

Now thread could be made so rapidly that spinners were forced to wait up for weavers. But not for long. In 1773, only three years after jenny was born, James Kay invented the flying shuttle.

Two years later, Richard Arkwright took out a second patent on his roller spinning frame. Run by water power, the spinning frame twisted threads tightly enough for them to be used as the strong warp threads of a loom. Warp threads go down the length of the loom. The flying shuttle carried the woof threads in and out among the warp threads across the loom.

Cloth could now be made by machine. The Industrial Revolution was well on its way.

Another Englishman, Samuel Crompton, contributed an additional improvement. Crompton's spinning "mule" drew fibers exquisitely long and fine. Then it wound these slender threads around spindles. Now machines could make fabrics as soft and delicate as those spun by the most nimble fingers.

New as industry was to America and new as America was to the world in 1793, an American, Eli Whitney, created a machine that changed history.

Whitney's cotton gin needed only a horse and one man to do the work of fifty men. It separated cotton fibers from their seed coverings. With a machine to take over the long, tedious labor of so many people, southern planters realized that they could now plant lots more cotton. There was still plenty of land available and they hurried to buy it up. Plantations grew huge.

But, although it had been easy to find land, it was not so easy to find people to work it. More than ever, plantations needed farm hands to plow the land, plant the seed and harvest the crop. They needed workers to bale the cotton and ship it up North where the new factories were.

The South found its answer in slave labor.

Plantation owners had been using slaves all along. In fact, an important use of the schooners built in New Eng-

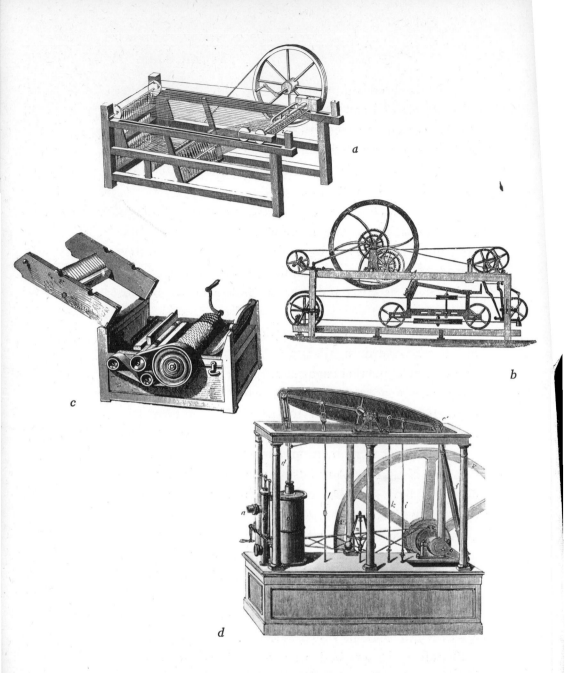

(a) The spinning jenny; (b) the spinning "mule"; (c) the cotton gin; (d) a steam engine for rotary machines

land was to bring free black people from Africa and sell them into slavery in America. Now that there was more land to be farmed, more cotton to be sold, more money to be made, southern plantation owners grew more greedy to own even more slaves. And even greedier to keep them.

Slavery might have died a natural death in America if the cotton gin hadn't made it possible to own so much land and get so rich. Now if slavery were abolished, plantation owners would be forced to pay farm workers. They would be forced to sell off parts of their huge plantations. Their profits would be much, much less.

Slavery was simply too profitable to give up. It could no longer die a natural death. It took a war to kill it.

Up north, in New England, where the land had been so unfriendly to farmers, it put its welcome mat out for industry. New England was dotted with tumbling brooks, rivers and waterfalls that could be harnessed as water power for the new machines. Enterprising businessmen set up little textile factories along the banks of these streams.

Some weavers gave up their farms and moved close to the new factories. Towns were born. Next to each of the new textile mills stood a new town.

Life was very different for the families who had once had their own cottage industries.

Now Papa was gone all day, working at a weaving machine. The older boys went out to work, too. There were only the women and children left at home to care for the house and the land. Children whose families moved to one of the new towns didn't even have their regular farm chores to do. There was no need any more for them to learn spinning and weaving from their parents. Now machines could do all that.

Now that there was less work at home for the children, people began to talk of building more schools. All children should learn to read and write, they said. After all, with the new machines, people would find their leisure time boring unless they could read.

While government officials were debating about building new schools, a brand new invention came along and changed everything.

James Watt, who had already invented several types of steam-driven engines, devised a way to use steam on rotary machines. In his first engines, Watt used steam to force a piston up and down. This was fine for pumping wells, but it didn't do much for other industries. When he discovered how to use steam power to turn wheels, he changed every industry.

Factories grew. They were no longer dependent on water power. Although the new towns grew along with the factories, other changes were not dramatic.

At first, in fact, machinery brought higher wages for the spinners and weavers, since it brought great prosperity to the entire textile industry. Northern factories could use more of the South's home-grown cotton. Manufacture of cotton goods expanded. Cartwright's mule produced a muslin so fine there was a constant demand for it—to make ladies' dresses and babies' clothes, for fine men's shirts and delicate curtains, for petticoats and ball gowns. The demand grew so large that, as one workman put it, "Old barns, cart-houses, out-buildings of all kinds were repaired, windows broke through the old blank walls, and all fitted up for the new loom-shops; weavers with new loom-shops arose in every direction. . . ."

Steam engines also made it possible to get raw materials to factories and manufactured goods back out into the rural South and West. Steam drove the railroad engines. Steam drove the canal boats and the Mississippi River boats. Steam worked the engines that helped mine the coal which was burned to create steam for other engines.

The power loom, originally invented by several Englishmen, was perfected by two Americans in 1814. Now, from ginning the cotton to weaving it, everything could be done by machine.

When mills were first built, the owners were likely to be weavers or carpenters or craftsmen themselves. Perhaps they'd had a bit of luck or a better head for business. That's how they got to be owners. But they worked alongside their men and took pride in their work. They knew their workers and what sort of lives they led. If a worker had to stay out because his wife was having a baby, the owner knew all about it. And he didn't dock the new father a day's pay for a day's work not done.

With each new invention, factories grew larger and this friendly atmosphere faded.

Machines were expensive. It took quite a lot of money to buy all the machines a large factory required. Rich men, with money to invest, were able to build enormous factories, employing as many as a thousand people. A man was said to invest his "capital," the money he didn't need for everyday living, in order to make more money. It's plain that if a man makes a profit on manufacturing twenty shirts, his profit will be even greater if he manufactures twenty thousand. The bigger the factory, the more workers it has, the bigger the profit.

Few of these rich men had ever been craftsmen themselves. Most had some capital and they enjoyed making profits. The capitalists invested their money in factories which machine-produced thousands and thousands of identical items in a process known as "mass production." They made huge fortunes and lived in splendid homes quite far from the noisy, ugly factories they owned and the squalid, filthy towns that grew up around the mills. Some owners, finding America simply too vulgar for their refined tastes, chose to live in Europe. Since they employed thousands of people, they couldn't be expected to know any one of them, much less be interested when one of the mill hands had a new baby.

Capitalists invested their money expecting to make good profits. And they did. America was a great big growing land that needed all the manufactured goods it could get and had plenty of raw materials to offer.

After a while the mill owners grew accustomed to making good profits. They began to want more. Soon they discovered any number of ways to get even bigger profits from their mills. One way was to own the houses the workers lived in. Then the mill hands would be forced to pay back part of what they earned to the mill owners in the form of rent. Another way was to own the stores where the mill hands shopped.

Now if they could only find a way to pay workers less. The mill hands certainly didn't deserve to earn much. Why, this new machinery was so simple to operate, a child could do it.

Chapter Three

OUT TO WORK

At first it seemed so splendid, going to work in the morning with Papa. Tucking a bit of lunch into a pocket, just as Papa always did. Then, at night, walking home beside the other men, feeling tall and proud and grown-up at last.

At home Mama would be waiting to serve dinner. As soon as the factory whistle blew "quitting time," she'd have gotten busy with her pots and pans, lit the stove, looked to the stew. She knew the workers would soon be home, tired and hungry after their long day at the mill. It was nice to be treated like a grown-up by Mama, too. Fussed over. Catered to.

But the best part of all was Saturday. Saturday was payday. Papa and everyone else in the family who worked at the mill handed all his pay over to Mama. The dollar bills and the change. It was a good feeling. Helping Mama was a very good feeling. It was hard to watch her worry when there wasn't enough food in the house. Then she would rock the babies, but they wouldn't sleep. They were too hungry to sleep. She would rock and rock but still they would cry. That's why it felt so good to give the week's wages to Mama.

But how long could this good feeling last? Day after day, the work grew harder until the mill loomed like an ugly jail that swallowed up all childhood.

The mill children were awakened by shrill blasts from the factory whistles at five in the morning. There was just enough time to hurry. A splash of cold water to the face, breakfast in one pocket, lunch in another, the mill children ran through the cold dark to the waiting machines.

At six o'clock the whistles shrieked again. Time for the work day to begin. The gates were shut. Locked against latecomers, oversleepers, the slow or the tired ones. Anyone who came a minute or two late lost an hour's pay.

Some children worked at the spinning machines. Some worked as bobbin boys, rolling bushels of bobbins from room to room. Some oiled the machines. Others moved supplies from place to place, preparing work for the skilled weavers.

At eight o'clock, they were permitted fifteen minutes for breakfast. At noon, half an hour for lunch.

Twelve hours a day, six days a week, the children fed the endless, ravening hunger of the machines. Machines which were never tired, never sleepy, never sick. Nothing could stop the swift shuttles as they hurled themselves across the looms. And the children raced to keep up. Anyone who couldn't keep up was out. Out of a job. If the machines went faster, hands went faster. And eyes. The mechanical mouths were not choosy about what they ate.

They would just as soon munch on a strand of hair as a silk thread from the bobbins.

Little girls must not bend too closely over their work. A lock of hair could easily get caught in the whirring wheels. It took just a moment for the machine to pull the hair and a piece of scalp from a child's head. It was not an uncommon accident.

Thin, small hands could fit into narrow places where grown-up fingers were too thick to go. But the little fingers must be swift and sure or the machine would catch them.

The mill child must be careful. Must be fast. There were plenty more outside the gate who would gladly exchange the singsong chant of playground games for the whirring, clanging roar of the machines. Noise that never stopped. From six until six, six days a week, it shrilled against their ears.

The mill child stood all day. His feet were tired. His ears ached. Or was it his eyes? Or his head? It was hard to tell. Perhaps it was the cold that made his body throb. It was so dark and so cold in the mill. The little ones, the really little ones, the seven- and eight-year-olds had to be watched over by the older ones or they might fall asleep standing up.

They came home too tired to eat the food their money bought. And often they fell asleep with their clothes still on. When the five o'clock whistle blew, they went back to the mill, without having seen the sun, the light of day or anything but the mill for twenty-four hours.

Older children sometimes earned as much as three or four dollars for a full week's work. Younger ones earned

The mill child would stand all day and then come home too tired to eat the food his money bought

less. A dollar was more than enough for them, the mill manager decided. After all, wasn't he actually doing *them* a favor? Getting them off the streets? Working in the mill, his greedy mind reasoned, the children would learn the value of money and good hard labor. They would be kept busy and out of trouble.

Twelve or thirteen hours a day, six days a week at the

mills and church on Sundays didn't leave much time for learning bad habits. Or anything else, for that matter.

Many foremen actually saw themselves as keepers of the morals of the children in their mills. They kept the children virtuous, pure and God-fearing with the help of a cat-o'-nine-tails. If a child seemed too quick to joke or too slow to work, out came the whip.

At first the mill children went to work with Papa. Later on it was Mama. And finally it was often only the children themselves who went to work.

Mill owners had discovered that women and children were willing to work for less money than men. When the man in the family worked, his wife and children thought of their earnings as "extra," and were willing to take less money for the same job.

But if the women and children did the job just as well and for less money, why not fire the men? Which is exactly what many mill owners did. A man, accustomed to earning seven dollars a week as a spinner, might arrive at the mill one day to find himself replaced by a ten-year-old girl. She was paid a dollar fifty for the same work.

Families began to live off their children's earnings. They had no other money. They could barely survive on the children's pay. Desperate parents sent younger and younger children to work in the mills. It took five to six working children to bring home one man's pay.

During the years when American industry was beginning to flourish, many European countries were suffering from severe famines. In Ireland, for several years in a row, the crop farmers counted on most failed. If there was no

The children began to pour through the factory gates when the mill owners discovered that the children would work for less money than their parents

Irish potato crop, there was nothing to eat in Ireland. In Italy and northern Europe, there were too many mouths to feed. The soil was simply too tired to produce the huge harvests needed to feed so many.

European peasants were starving to death. If they could only get to America, they believed they could find work.

Hundreds of thousands of Europeans began to immigrate to America every year.

Newly arrived immigrants, docking at Boston and New York harbors, were urged to head for the mills where they would find "good homes, good pay."

Wagons were sent into the countryside to recruit young

farm girls. They were promised freedom and adventure and high wages to spend on pretty clothes.

It didn't take long for these wagons to be known as "slavers."

The labor force grew. Mill owners were able to pick and choose among the workers. Naturally, they continued to pick women and children since they could pay them less.

Though some states had laws which prohibited young children from working, hardly anyone paid attention to these laws. Mill owners ignored them. Foremen ignored them. Impoverished parents were forced to ignore them. In fact, there was generally some helpful "friend" who could teach a family how to get around the law. Particularly immigrant families. They were really puzzled. They had expected to find work in America. But what sort of place was this where fathers stayed home and sent their

Europeans came by the thousands every year—many to work in the mills

young children off to the mills? It took someone from the "old country" who could speak their language to explain it to them.

And that's whom the foremen hired and the mill owners used—someone from the "old country."

Looking prosperous and well-fed, a fellow immigrant would visit newly arrived families. Just being friendly, of course. He would sympathize with their problems and the difficulty Papa had in finding work. And then, looking toward the older children, he'd wonder out loud what *they* were doing at home. How come they weren't in the mills, helping their families as other children did?

When Mama or Papa explained that none of the children had reached his fourteenth birthday yet, their new "friend" took the immigrant family under his wing. There were so many ways to get around the law, he would explain to them. With a well-placed dollar here or there, he could help them get forged papers that passed a ten- or eleven-year-old as fourteen. And if an eight- or nine-year-old were tall for his age, perhaps that, too, could be arranged. Their generous "friend" from the old country would even lend them the money to get the forged papers. The children could pay him back once they started to work. Each week they could pay back some part of the loan, plus interest on the loan, of course. After all, he couldn't be expected to do such favors for nothing.

So the "slaver" earned his money from both sides at once. From the owners, he got money for finding cheap labor. From the workers, he got money for finding work.

A reporter wrote of seeing "a child of five years working at night." The Reverend Edgar Gardner Murphy took pictures of "little children of six and seven years who were at work for twelve or thirteen hours a day" in textile mills.

But grown men couldn't find work. "Husky, able-bodied men would steal by the watchmen and get into the mill, and then beg for a job where they could make any wages at all," an article in *The American Magazine* stated. "There are many able-bodied men today in the mills doing children's jobs, taking children's places and receiving the pitiful children's wages."

Dr. Elizabeth Shapleigh, practicing medicine in Lawrence, Massachusetts, held an extremely revolutionary point of view for those days. She believed young children should be in school and not at work. She knew the mill children. She treated them when they sickened, and she was often forced to watch them die.

"A considerable number of these boys and girls," Dr. Shapleigh wrote, "die within the first two or three years after beginning work. Thirty-six out of every one hundred of all men and women who work in the mill die before or by the time they are twenty-five years of age."

One of the cotton mills, built in a hurry to house machines and never mind the people, simply collapsed. Six hundred and seventy men, women and children were buried in the ruins. Hours later the heap of wreckage began to smolder. Crackling fingers of fire flew into flames. Hundreds more were burned to death. An investigating committee found "defective pillars . . . the primary cause of the disaster."

Once-hopeful immigrants, "rosy-cheeked maidens" whisked by "slavers" from their peaceful New England farms, were all but smothered in hopeless despair.

Chapter Four

SLAVES OF
BIG BUSINESS

By the middle of the nineteenth century a transcontinental railroad had been built to connect the east and west coasts of America. Gold had been discovered in California. The land west of the Mississippi River no longer belonged to free-roaming cowboys and Indians. It had been fenced in, bridled, tamed and planted in orderly wheat fields.

Villages had become cities. Cities had become industrial centers. The roar of machinery was heard across the land. America had new leaders who would soon become the new aristocracy of the nation. Just as rich farmers used to be known as "lords of the manor," almost as though they were titled noblemen, the new capitalists were known as "barons of industry."

Using imagination and intelligence to organize men and materials, the "barons" were the first to see the marvels possible through large-scale production. Machine-made clothes, bricks, tools, furniture were all better and cheaper. Work that had been backbreaking labor for men was accomplished swiftly and cheaply by machines.

Some people, once accustomed to rough woolen clothes, were wearing silks. Fashionable ladies hired French teachers and dancing masters to help them acquire a greater delicacy of manner. They couldn't bear the idea of being laughed at as "crude Americans." Wives of well-to-do businessmen, or even "barons," they tried to play their new roles with all the elegance and charm they imagined a real European baroness would display.

By the middle of the nineteenth century, the rough New World had begun to acquire a shiny, smooth surface finish. But it was only the thinnest sort of surface finish. Below the surface, life for the majority of the people was rougher than ever.

In the South, no slave child was too young to be separated from his mother and sold to another owner. Nor was any child of a slave too young to pick cotton or feel the lash of the overseer's whip if he didn't work fast enough.

Hungry mills in the North were swallowing up cotton as fast as the South could grow it. Improvements on Eli Whitney's cotton gin made it possible for a slave to clean a thousand pounds of cotton a day. Before the gin, it was considered a good day's work to clean one pound. With a crude gin, a slave could clean fifty pounds a day. After the gin was harnessed to steam, one slave could produce a thousand times as much clean cotton in one day as he could before the gin.

Naturally, the profit to the plantation owner was much higher. And just as naturally, each slave was almost a thousand times more valuable to his master. No wonder the South refused to give up slavery.

Slaves and owners, like northern workers and their employers, had once had something in common. They had been held together by a common interest in the work they did. They knew each other and they knew each other's families. But the machines, and the huge profits that came with them, changed all that.

Just as northern manufacturers treated workers as mere tools, useful for making money, cotton planters thought of slaves as animals to be worked until they dropped. Overseers were put in charge of enormous work gangs. An overseer was expected to produce a certain amount of cotton each year, no matter what. Like the foreman in a northern mill, the southern overseer was simply at the head of the human working machine. If the human machine didn't work well, foremen and overseers lost their jobs. It was as simple as that.

But it was not so simple for people to learn to think of themselves as machines. No matter how driven they were by foremen or overseers, people kept right on having human feelings. They kept right on having families and worrying about them. And as conditions grew more and more painful for the poorest people, a handful of observers grew more and more concerned.

Abolitionists demanded that all slaves be freed. It was immoral for a few men to grow rich on the labor of so many, they argued. Northern manufacturers agreed. Their system, they pointed out, was based on "free labor," not "slave power."

Congressman William H. Seward of New York described the situation. "This class of slaveholders," he

TYRANNY AND FREEDOM
OR
THE ROMANCE OF CHILD LABOR

The "barons of industry" were the first to see the marvels possible
through large-scale production and the use of little children

wrote, "consisting of only three hundred and forty-seven thousand persons, own more than three million other persons who are denied all civil and political rights, and freedom of speech, freedom of the ballot box, freedom of education, freedom of literature and freedom of popular assemblies. . . . The slaveholding class has become the governing power in each of the slaveholding states. . . ."

Seward predicted that a clash between the two opposing systems of "free labor" and "slave labor" was inevitable. The war that would result, he declared, was not "accidental, unnecessary, the work of interested or fanatical agitators. . . ." Instead, he insisted, "It is an irrepressible conflict between opposing and enduring forces."

It's a little difficult to believe that northern mill owners, who were mercilessly abusing children for profit, felt such pure moral indignation at slavery.

Actually, their objections were far from pure. It was their profits they were concerned with. Cotton grown in the South was being sold for manufacture in England. In some cases, English manufacturers were able to produce fabrics more cheaply than American manufacturers. Afraid of this competition, northern mill owners wanted tariffs imposed on English goods. Southern Congressmen opposed these taxes, because they knew the English would retaliate by refusing to buy their cotton.

The South wanted to keep its profits.

The North wanted to keep its profits.

If slavery were abolished, cotton would go up in price and English manufacturers might buy elsewhere, Southerners feared.

Their fears were correct. Four bloody years later, the civil

War was over. The Union was preserved. Slavery was abolished.

And still there was cause for concern. North and South, freed slaves and free workers still lived in the most abject misery.

Still younger children were being sent to work in the mills. Still more industries were discovering how useful and cheap young children could be. In coal mines, in glass factories, in canneries, in the "street trades," as newsboys, boot blacks, food vendors, little children were helping big men make big profits.

Now new voices began to be heard. Just as the abolitionists had felt concern over slavery, some Americans began to feel concern over the young "wage slaves." Their consciences would not permit them to enjoy cheap and plentiful goods produced at such enormous human cost.

Some were ministers. Some were teachers. Some were writers. And some were well-educated young ladies from well-to-do homes. They were young women who couldn't be expected to have the vaguest idea of what it meant to be a mill child. Yet, somehow, they escaped their embroidery and permitted themselves to see the truth.

Perhaps, in doing an errand for their ministers, they were asked to drop off a parcel of food for a sick child.

Perhaps, looking for their favorite milliner, they got lost in town one day and happened on the hideous slums where mill people lived.

Perhaps they wondered where the money for their fine clothes and lovely homes came from and went to have a look at the mill itself.

The world has always seemed to be blessed with a special group of people who are not afraid to ask questions. They use their eyes and their ears, their feet and their heads to find the answers. And once they know what's wrong and why, they're ready to work for change. They're not likely to throw up their hands in despair and say, "Oh, that's life." Or, "You can't change human nature." What they do is roll up their sleeves and get to work.

Jane Addams, Lillian Wald, Florence Kelley were just such young women from just such well-to-do homes. And they served as inspiration to hundreds of others.

Robert Hunter, John Spargo, Jacob Riis were writers whose voices would not be stilled. Through them, America heard the cries of the working children.

The Reverend Edgar Gardner Murphy and other militant clergymen did more than comfort the poor. From their pulpits they spoke to stir people's consciences.

They told America that as early as 1791, when Samuel Slater built the first mill in America, his spinning machines were run by nine little children, who worked fourteen hours a day, six days a week. President Andrew Jackson called Sam Slater the "father of American manufacturers." Ten years later, Father Slater's mills employed over a hundred children. The oldest was ten. The youngest was four.

They told America that in 1832 a convention of New England working men estimated that two-fifths of all the people employed in manufacturing were children.

They told America that the situation was not getting

Child workers in Port Royal, South Carolina

better. That every year it grew uglier and more frightening.

A young Frenchman, Michel Chevalier, visited America in 1834 and sent home a strangely glowing report on one of America's mill towns. True, Lowell, Massachusetts, was different from other mill towns. For one thing, it employed *only* women and young children. For another, it was supposedly set up as an ideal town—a Utopian mill town.

But, in fact, it was built for the most practical reason, to make money for its owner.

Francis Cabot Lowell, son of a wealthy New England merchant family, set up the first factory system for the manufacturing of cloth in America. He built not only the factories, but the entire town in which the workers lived. He built dormitories and churches, shops and boarding houses. And he had an original scheme about how to hold on to his labor force. He would hire and train only very young women to run his machines.

Since it was commonly thought that young girls who were not constantly kept busy would fall prey to temptation and wickedness, Lowell presented his plan as a favor to their parents. Girls were just a financial drain on their families and a burden to society, anyhow.

Lowell's mills would keep them busy at least seventy hours a week. Respectable women were hired as kind of "house mothers" to see that the girls lived good, clean lives and went to church on Sundays.

In 1835, Harriet Martineau, an English writer, was well impressed with Lowell's experiment.

"I visited the corporate factory establishment at Waltham, within a few miles of Boston. . . . Five hundred persons were employed at the time of my visit. The girls earn two and some, three, dollars a week, besides their board. The little children earn one dollar a week. . . .

"The people work about seventy hours a week, on the average. The time of work varies with the length of the days. . . . The health is good; or rather (as this is too much to be said about health anywhere in the United States), it is no worse than it is elsewhere."

What Harriet Martineau meant when she wrote, "The time of work varies with the length of days," was that the girls worked from sunrise to sunset.

The Massachusetts legislature investigating the hours of children in factories reported, "It appears that the time of employment is generally twelve or thirteen hours a day, excepting Sabbath, which leaves little time for instruction."

Thirty years later, Michel Chevalier was a dignitary in the French government in charge of the 1867 World's Fair. He still had his pleasant memories of Lowell and decided it would be interesting to set up a model village at the Paris fair. He wrote to Senator Sumner of Massachusetts, asking to have a group of young girls from Lowell sent to Paris with their looms so that visitors to the exposition, seeing them at work, would feel as though they were actually visiting Lowell.

But Michel Chevalier's memories were thirty years old. The mills had grown. The neat little, new little houses had turned into dirty, crowded slums. No delegation of girls from Lowell went to the Paris fair to show the world the wonders they could produce from their looms. Instead, on April 1, the day the exposition was opened by Emperor Bonaparte of France, the Lowell girls went out on strike for a shorter working day.

Charles Douglass, president of the New England Association of Farmers, Mechanics and Other Working Men, described quite a different Lowell from Harriet Martineau's.

He reported that four thousand young women and children were "dragging out a life of slavery and wretchedness." He spoke of "their woe-stricken appearance. These establishments are the present abode of wretchedness, disease, and misery; and are invariably calculated to perpetuate them—if not destroy liberty itself!"

Douglass did not mince words. "The sons of our farmers," he told Americans, "as soon as they are of sufficient age, have been induced to hasten off to the factory, where . . . they are taught to become willing servants, the servile instruments of their employers' oppression and extortion."

By 1881, only seven states had passed laws that children must reach at least the age of twelve before they could be employed. And the only proof of age required was the parents' word.

In 1881, a young girl named Jane Addams, visiting Europe as part of her education, was taken on a tour of London's East End. It was Saturday night, and because the markets would be closed on Sunday and the vegetables spoiled by Monday, peddlers were auctioning off their wares to the highest bidder.

"We saw two huge masses of ill-clad people clamoring around two hucksters' carts," she wrote. When one man won the rotted cabbage the crowd had been fighting over, "he instantly sat down on the curb, tore it with his teeth, and hastily devoured it, unwashed and uncooked as it was."

With horror, Jane Addams saw for the first time "pale faces dominated by that most unlovely of human expressions, the cunning and shrewdness of the bargain hunter who starves if he cannot make a successful trade . . . hands empty, clutching forward for food already unfit to eat."

On her return to America, she took a good look at the cities of her native land, at the slums and the mills of her own country. They were no better.

In 1881, Jacob Riis, newly arrived in America, wandered unemployed through New York City's slum streets, wondering where his next meal would come from.

In 1881, Marie and Bessie Von Vorst, two gentlewomen disguised as poor working girls, were trying to find out through personal experience what the life of a working child was really like.

Robert Hunter, Rev. Edgar Gardner Murphy, John Spargo, Everett Macy, Florence Kelley, the Von Vorst sisters, Jane Addams. Theirs would be the voices raised loudest in protest in the years to come.

Chapter Five

THE SETTLEMENT HOUSE MOVEMENT

O n Halsted Street, in the center of Chicago's sprawling, teeming slum section, stood the old Hull Mansion.

When millionaire Charles Hull first built his beautiful home in 1856, he chose the western side of Lake Michigan because he wanted to be out in the country. But as Chicago grew, the city became America's major railway center. Produce heading east, goods heading west, all rolled through Chicago. Western cattle were shipped to its huge slaughterhouses to be packaged and shipped out again. The stockyards made a million dollars a week and Chicago was America's second largest manufacturing city. Immigrants who landed on the East Coast and found the going too tough turned west to Chicago. By the end of the nineteenth century, two-thirds of Chicago's population was foreign born.

The western side of Lake Michigan was no longer millionaires' row. The old mansions were turned into rooming houses where entire families huddled together in one room. Halsted Street was crowded with pushcarts and people. It reeked of garbage the city didn't even bother to collect and of the slaughterhouses nearby.

Children still too young for school, whose mothers worked twelve hours each day, drifted aimlessly through the streets. Others, too young to be finished with school, were already at work in tenement sweatshops.

Here in the middle of Chicago's worst slum, between a saloon and a funeral parlor, Jane Addams found exactly the home she'd been looking for. It was Charles Hull's old mansion. But now, it looked just like the rest of the neighborhood, seedy, run-down, a slum. It took some imagination to see that the house could be restored and made lovely again. Friends thought Jane was mad, but she could see that it was a good old building. It needed repairs. It had gone through many hands. But it was still spacious. It still had its wide halls and open fireplaces. Here, in the old Hull mansion, Jane decided to establish America's first settlement house.

The repairs were made and Jane Addams moved in. She furnished the house lovingly with pictures collected in Europe and "a few bits of family mahogany." Her neighbors were startled at the appearance of Hull House's new tenants. Jane Addams and her friend and coworker, Ellen Starr, were obviously well-to-do young women. Whatever could they be thinking of, moving right into the heart of Chicago's southwest slum district? Not only the neighbors, but all of Chicago soon found out.

Jane Addams had a perfectly clear goal in mind. She wanted to create a community center, like Toynbee Hall

Jane Addams, founder of Hull House

in London, which would act as teacher, family and friend to the immigrants who had left all those ties behind them in Europe. She wanted to provide a place where the poor could find help and the confused seek advice. She wanted to start a nursery school for children whose mothers worked, classes in English for the foreign born. Music, dance and art classes to open a new world of pleasure where there had been little but pain. She hoped to provide medical care and teach her neighbors something about sanitary conditions. The death rate in those slums was appalling. She wanted to keep the people alive and, more than that, to make their lives worth living.

In the days before the establishment of government agencies to help the sick, the old and the poor, all social work was done by volunteers. Though there was an urgent need for a more organized system, few people were yet aware of it. Jane had first realized how urgent the need was when she saw starving children grovel for food in London's East End.

She could see that in the days before the industrial revolution, people had not been so isolated from each other. Their lives had been woven together into a fabric of communal interdependence. When, in 1899, a Congressional committee inquired into the changes this quiet revolution had brought about, one witness gave them this eloquent description:

"In these old shops, years ago, one man owned the shop; he took in work and three, four, five, or six others, neighbors, came in there and sat down and made shoes right in their laps, and there was no machinery. Everybody was at liberty to talk; they were all politicians. . . . Of course, under these conditions, there was absolute freedom and exchange of ideas, they naturally would become more intelligent than shoe workers can at the present time, when they are driving each man to see how many shoes he can handle, and where he is surrounded by noisy machinery. And another thing, this nervous strain on a man doing just one thing over and over again must necessarily have a wearing effect on him and his ideals, I believe, must be lowered."

Since there were over one hundred subdivisions in the making of a shoe in these new mass-production factories, the worker, according to this same witness, "becomes a mere machine."

The artisan no longer practiced "the gentle craft of leather." He had become the servant to the machine. There was no time now for the "freedom and exchange of ideas" artisans had enjoyed when "neighbors sat down and made shoes right in their laps." In those days, every man considered his ideas as important as anyone else's. If he disagreed with the neighbor in whose little shop he worked, he said so. And maybe they had a rousing good political argument. Why not? They both respected each other. Employer and employee were both skilled crafts-men, sitting side by side with shoes in their laps.

Of course, even in those days, there were some who were hired and some who did the hiring. There were rich farmers and poor farmers.

Still, a rich farmer up the road was sure to know if his poor neighbors were having troubles. And it was only neighborly to offer a bit of help. People were able to count on each other. Someone you helped would one day help someone else. Perhaps it would be you. Perhaps not. It didn't matter. What did matter was the caring.

The rich farmer might have lands and barns and cattle, but when a new baby was coming he still needed the poor farmer's wife to help in the birthing. He knew he needed her and he could count on her. As she could count on him if her husband fell ill at harvest time. Even in the towns, which were then still quite small, a man had family, friends and neighbors. He was not alone.

All that had changed with the industrial revolution. Men's splendid inventions now ginned cotton, wove cloth, sewed boots. Good, useful things were made faster and better than anyone dreamed possible. The men who owned the machines and the factories grew richer every day. It was not so pleasant to live in crowded cities, teem-ing with strangers. They built their grand estates outside the cities, where the air was cleaner and there was room to keep horses for their children to ride. They heard of the art treasures in Italy, of the beauty of Paris and they travelled abroad. Little by little, they came to know less and less about the people who worked for them. They were no longer neighbors. A man could hardly be expected to keep up with the lives of thousands of employees. He looked out for himself. And they had better look out for themselves. He didn't need them. And they'd better not count on him.

Men who barely earned enough each day to keep their families clothed and fed couldn't hope to put money aside for an emergency. If a child fell ill, if the factory shut down, if a man could no longer work, he was destitute. Fear was a specter that haunted the lives of the poor. There was no way out. No place to turn. Where then would help come from, if help were needed?

Jane Addams knew that eventually the government must become the social agency through which change would come. She could see that as cities grew, individuals would be less and less able to keep up with the desperate needs of the slum dwellers. In some way, the government would have to curb the profits of the terribly rich. But how? Who was she to propose that laws be written putting an end to child labor, to unsafe working conditions, to greedy landlords renting out unlivable space? How could she convince the lawmakers that even the poor were entitled to clean streets, pure milk and unpolluted water? No doubt government officials would accuse her of sentimentality and ignorance. But if she demonstrated through Hull House that the despised poor flocked there to learn how to better themselves, could she still be accused of sentimentality? If she showed, through years of living and working in Chicago's worst slum area, that she had first-hand knowledge of its actual conditions, could she still be accused of ignorance? She doubted it.

When Jane Addams first discussed her plans for Hull House with her friend Ellen Starr she half expected to be laughed at. Instead, Ellen reacted with instant, joyous enthusiasm. Like many other privileged, upper-class girls, Ellen was fed up with her own passive, fruitless sort of existence. She travelled in Europe, visited art galleries, attended concerts, while all around her girls half her age were turning old from overwork. If they were only half alive, then so was she. The pursuit of pleasure had become a stifling bore, an endless round of nothing. To feel alive, she felt she must be useful.

Jane began to suspect that there might be many more American girls who shared Ellen's feeling. Girls who felt anguish at what they saw around them, but who had no idea of what could be done, or how. Hull House would be open to them, as well as to the poor. At Hull House, they could learn to work.

Those Hull House residents who received their first training in social work at America's first settlement house make up quite an impressive list of names.

There was Florence Kelley, a lifelong crusader for a permanent end to child labor, for women's rights, for the rights of all working people.

There were Sophinisba Breckenridge and Grace and Edith Abbott who made a science of collecting facts and writing them up accurately and unemotionally so that readers could come to their own conclusions. Today, sociologists rely quite a lot on this method of statistical survey, first introduced by Miss Breckenridge and the Abbott sisters. Because today, just as then, facts are hard to ignore. People who know them feel moved to act on them.

There was Dr. Alice Hamilton, America's first researcher in the field of occupational diseases. It was while working at Hull House that she first began to suspect that many of the illnesses she saw around her were caused by the work people did. Children who spent their days in airless mills and who went without food and sleep were ideal victims of the bacteria which caused tuberculosis.

Children who worked in match factories developed hideous, deformed chins. Matches were made of phosphorus. And phosphorus ate away at the children's flesh. "Phossy jaw" could be stopped simply by using another chemical in making matches.

Children developed silicosis, an incurable lung disease, from working in mines. Each breath they took filled their lungs with coal and dust instead of air.

Children in the steel mills were dying of gas poisoning. Dr. Hamilton proved that poisonous gases could be replaced by harmless ones. As a result of her work, the Occupational Disease Act was passed, regulating industrial use of chemicals. The Act guaranteed that employers would be held responsible if their carelessness caused injuries to their employees. They would have to pay the medical bills and compensate the workers for as long as they suffered.

Probably no amount of money in the world could really compensate for the misery of pretty young girls who ended up with "phossy jaws." But there was no other way to regulate big business except to cut into its profits. Barons of industry were far too removed from the lives of common people to feel responsibility for any harm that came to them. But they were quite close to their pocketbooks. When they were hit in the pocketbook, they felt pain. Most labor laws were eventually based on this fundamental idea, and enforced in the same way.

Julia Lathrop, another Hull House volunteer, was almost solely responsible for the first laws passed to protect dependent and neglected children.

A steady stream of some of the most remarkable men and women in America's history came out of Hull House.

Hull House itself became the model for settlement houses built in other cities throughout the country. Like Hull House, these settlements drew to them the finest and most conscientious young people in the land. Their deepest need was to help others. They wanted to be useful to society, even if that meant changing it.

Today, a student with the same goals would be very likely to go into social work. In that case, he would choose a college that offers courses in sociology and specializes in training social workers. Almost all colleges do. But in the early days of settlement work, the only place to learn how to help organize a community, change its laws and improve its conditions was the settlement house.

Jane Addams, Robert Hunter, Florence Kelley, Sophinisba Breckenridge and so many others who worked along

Hull House became the model for settlement houses throughout the country

with them were actually pioneers, opening a new frontier.

The idea they proposed was revolutionary. Since people could no longer count on their neighbors' helping hands, the government must be everyone's helping hand. Laws must be created to protect the young, the very old, the poor and the sick. The government had not played this role in people's lives before. It would not be easy to convince the country that it should begin now. But even "now" was too late as far as Jane Addams was concerned.

"Our very first Christmas at Hull House," she wrote, "when we knew nothing of child labor, a number of little girls refused the candy which was offered them as part of Christmas good cheer, saying simply that they 'worked in a candy factory and could not stand the sight of it.' We discovered that for six weeks they had worked from seven in the morning until nine at night and they were exhausted as well as satiated. This sharp awareness of economic conditions came in the midst of the season of good will."

Jane's horror of child labor had just begun. "During that same winter three boys from a Hull House club were injured at one machine in a neighboring factory for lack of a guard which would have cost but a few dollars. When the injury of one of these boys resulted in his death, we felt quite sure that the owners of the factory would share our horror and remorse, and that they would do everything possible to prevent the recurrence of such a tragedy. To our surprise, they did nothing whatever, and I made my first acquaintance with those pathetic documents signed by the parents of working children that they will make no claim for damages resulting from 'carelessness.' "

During the frequent visits that Jane and her fellow Hull House workers made to their neighbors, they "discovered women sewing upon sweatshop work, and often they were assisted by incredibly small children."

Jane remembered "a little girl of four who pulled out basting threads hour after hour, sitting at a stool at the feet of her mother, a little bunch of human misery."

"We learned," Jane wrote, "to know many families in which the working children contributed to the support of their parents, not only because they spoke English better than their immigrant parents and were willing to take lower wages, but because their parents gradually found it easier to live upon their earnings. A South Italian peasant who has picked olives and packed oranges from his toddling boyhood cannot see the difference between the outdoor healthy work he did and the long hours of monotonous factory life his child encounters when he goes to work in Chicago."

Later on, a father came to Hull House "in great grief over the death of his eldest child, a little girl of twelve, who had brought the largest wages into the family fund. In the midst of his genuine sorrow he said, 'She was the oldest kid I had. Now I have to go back to work again. . . .' " It was easier for the child to find work than the father.

"Another little girl of thirteen," Jane reported, "employed in a laundry at a heavy task beyond her strength, committed suicide, because she had borrowed three dollars from a companion which she could not repay unless she confided the story to her parents and gave up an entire week's wages—but what could the family live upon that week in case she did!"

At that time, there was no information to be had on just how many young children were employed in Chicago's industries.

An energetic young woman named Florence Kelley, one of Hull House's residents, decided to take the problem to the Illinois State Bureau of Labor. She suggested that they do a thorough investigation of child labor in Chicago. Her special target was the "sweating system."

This was a particularly vicious system for exploiting young children. A factory with many large orders to fill would often find it difficult to get the work out on time. In that case, it would hand over cartons of half-finished garments to a middleman. The middleman found workers to finish the garments at home. In that way, the factory owner got the work done without providing space and light and heat for a great many workers.

The middleman, or "sweater," knew just where to find people so desperate for work that they would work for almost no money at all. Women with young children to care for could not leave their homes. The more children they had, the more tied they were to their homes. The more children they had, the more they needed the work. The more children they had, the more hands they had to work with them.

The factory owner paid the sweater for the number of "pieces," or garments, he delivered finished. The sweater paid the people who did the finishing for him. The difference between what he was paid and what he paid out was the sweater's profit. Naturally, he kept his profits as high as he could.

Sometimes the sweater had the women and children all come to work in his own slum apartment. Sometimes he let them do the work in their own. These slums were so filthy, the women and children working in them so desperate, they came to be known as "sweat shops." Places where a worker sweated out every penny paid to him.

Under the "sweating system" it was impossible to know just how many children in how many homes were working how many hours a day. Nor was it possible to know how old they were. Nor how little they earned.

Florence Kelley suggested that the Illinois State Bureau of Labor investigate the sweating system and they, in turn, hired her to do the investigating.

Mrs. Kelley, with the help of other Hull House residents,

covered the neighborhood on foot, knocking on doors, walking to the top floors of tenement slums, asking questions, collecting facts. They put together the first actual, factual, statistical information on child labor in Chicago.

The facts were so shocking, the committee recommended that the legislature of Illinois take a hand in the matter. They urged the legislature to pass a law regulating the sanitary conditions of sweat shops and making it illegal to employ a child younger than fourteen years of age.

The suggestions of the committee, headed by Florence Kelley, later became the provisions of the first factory law of Illinois. But it took some time and plenty of persuasion before the law was passed.

Before Mrs. Kelley could persuade the legislature, she and Jane Addams realized they would need to have public opinion behind them. The most important labor union in Chicago at the time, the Trades and Labor Assembly, immediately gave its support. Now they wanted and needed the support of the women's clubs and the more prosperous and powerful citizens. If some of these people just knew the facts, Jane felt, some would be stirred by their consciences to support the passage of the bill.

"A little group of us," Jane remembered, "addressed meetings of trade unions, benefit societies, church organizations, and social clubs literally every evening for three months."

Although Hull House had been in existence only three years, Jane and her fellow workers had collected a staggering set of facts. They also drew from their own day-to-day experiences, living as they did in the heart of the slum

A family making artificial flowers in their apartment

area, to convince audiences that the government must act to limit child labor. They railed against factory night work for young girls and were able to point out that one of these factories was close by Hull House. They had seen with their own eyes these "pale, listless girls in the early morning hours as they returned from work, debilitated and exhausted. . . ."

"A conscientious girl finds it hard to sleep," Jane told the well-dressed ladies of the women's clubs, "with her mother washing and scrubbing within a few feet of her bed."

The people were convinced. They put pressure on the State legislature to pass the first labor bill. But there was too much opposition from big business. A year later the State Supreme Court declared the law unconstitutional.

"The bitterest opposition," Jane wrote, "came from the large glass companies, who were so accustomed to use the labor of children that they were convinced the manufacturing of glass could not be carried on without it."

The labor bill had received its most enthusiastic reception from the trade unions. Jane began to see that although laws could state the conditions under which people should work, it took trade unions to see that the laws were obeyed.

Hull House workers were to learn over the years that they would almost always be able to work hand in hand with the trade unions. At the beginning, some union leaders were suspicious of these "do-gooder" ladies. They suspected them of enjoying their little adventure on the wrong side of the tracks. They were sure that when the going got really rough, the ladies would go back to their needlepoint.

But it never happened.

For the rest of her life, Jane Addams remained dedicated to the workingman's cause.

Hull House continued to train young people in the ways to fight for change.

Florence Kelley went on from Hull House to become head of the National Consumers' League, an organization which did not stop battling child labor until the battle was just about won. It was Mrs. Kelley who trained Frances Perkins, the first woman member of a U.S. President's cabinet. Mrs. Perkins was Secretary of Labor under Franklin D. Roosevelt.

Sophinisba Breckenridge was responsible for the training of countless social workers. As an outgrowth of her work at Hull House, she helped found America's first school of social work at the University of Chicago. There, two other Hull House graduates, Grace and Edith Abbott, did their pioneer studies, *Women and Children as Wage Earners in the United States.*

John R. Commons, whose four-volume *History of Labor in the United States* is considered the classic work on this subject, trained at Hull House. Philosopher John Dewey trained at Hull House. People helped change history at Hull House.

In 1903 the Illinois legislature passed a child labor law which, according to historians, "contained pioneer provisions." These same historians saw Jane Addams as "the leading personality in the campaign waged to pass the law." The Illinois Industrial Commission of the State Federation of Woman's Clubs and the Cook County Child Saving League "were the leading organizations in support of the bill." Both of these organizations stemmed directly from the work at Hull House.

Chapter Six

THE SOUTH:
AFTER THE SLAVE,
THE CHILD

Though several northern states had passed extremely weak child labor laws by the turn of the century, there was still no southern state which controlled child labor.

The child labor movement first appeared in the South where the cotton textile industry was expanding rapidly. In just the ten years from 1890 to 1900, the number of textile workers in southern mills tripled. In 1890, when 25 per cent of these southern textile mill workers were children under the age of sixteen, no one seemed to be very troubled about it. But in 1900, when 25 per cent amounted to twenty-five thousand children, the consciences of some citizens became aroused. They grew even more concerned when a United States Industrial Commission report testified that "many children worked at the age of eight." Of course, this meant that those children never learned to read or write.

Not only were they spending their entire childhood in filthy, ugly mills, indoors, away from the sun and air. But without education, they were trapped into spending their adult lives in the very same way, in those very same mills. Those who survived, that is. Because scurvy, tuberculosis, pneumonia, silicosis, malnutrition took many of the children before they even reached their teens.

The South had suffered terribly during the Civil War. Many Southerners' farms were ruined, their homes burned, their back yards were turned into battlefields. But the greatest blow of all was the loss of their young men. Close to seventy-five thousand Confederate soldiers were killed during the Civil War.

For a long time afterward, the entire South seemed to be sunk in apathy. It was as though they didn't expect to recover and couldn't care less. The economic system on which they had lived had been abolished. Southern planters could no longer become rich on the free labor of slaves.

A handful of southern businessmen, with more imagination than most, could see that the South would have to change its entire way of life. It would have to change from an agricultural society to an industrial one. Or else starve to death.

Since cotton grew in the South and was ginned in the South, why shouldn't thread be spun and cloth woven in the South, these businessmen argued. It didn't take long for other businessmen to realize how right they were. From 1880 to 1900, the volume of goods manufactured in the South grew from less than $458,000,000 worth of factory products to $1,463,000,000. This was an increase of 220 per cent.

The South pulled itself out of its apathy. Once the

patient began to recover, there was no lingering convalescence. One day moaning and groaning in bed, the next, out in the ball park, playing. How did they do it?

Naturally, there were many reasons. Imaginative, ambitious businessmen. A marvelous supply of raw materials, right at hand. A ready market for their manufactured products. But most historians agree with the well-known economist who said that the single most important factor in the swift, immense industrial development of the South was "chiefly . . . her supplies of tractable and cheap labor."

During the same period, from 1880 to 1900, the proportion of child workers in cotton mills outside the South actually decreased somewhat. In the South it remained at 25 per cent.

In 1906, it was reported that at least sixty thousand children under fourteen years of age were employed in southern textile mills. Observers who went into the mills, to see conditions for themselves, estimated that at least half of the mill children were under twelve.

Jane Addams writes of finding a child of five doing night work in a South Carolina mill.

The Reverend Edgar Gardner Murphy photographed "little children of six and seven years who were at work for twelve and thirteen hours a day in Alabama mills. In Columbia, South Carolina, and Montgomery, Alabama, there are hundreds of little children who do not appear to be more than nine or ten years of age, at work in the mills, by night as well as day."

Reverend Murphy was the man with a conscience who did most to arouse the thinking, feeling people of the

South. He was a Protestant Episcopal minister in Montgomery, Alabama.

Like Jane Addams, he spent almost every evening talking to groups of people. He told them what he had seen with his own eyes. He showed them the photographs he himself had taken in the mills. Sometimes there was not a dry eye in the house when Rev. Murphy left the platform. But it was not their tears that Edgar Gardner Murphy wanted. It was action.

He begged his audiences to agitate for child labor laws.

He organized the Alabama Child Labor Committee. He convinced newspaper owners in several cities to expose the real story of what was happening in the South's "wonderful new mills."

"These miracles of modern industry" were finally bringing prosperity to a very small part of the population.

But more than one reporter plainly told readers where their money was coming from. Profits were high, industry was able to grow at lightning speed "from the enslavement of children."

One outraged reporter, after having been taken by Reverend Murphy to see night work at the mills, wrote:

"These 'poor whites,' as they are expressively called, even by their Negro neighbors, have for many years eked out a scanty living upon their farms, all the members of the family uniting in the struggle against nature. Drawn into the current of the new industrial order, they do not realize that, even though children worked hard upon the farms, there is an immense difference between the dust-laden air of a factory and the pure air of a farm; between the variety of tasks of farm life with the endless opportu-

nities for change and individual initiative, and the strained
attention and monotonous tasks of mill life. . . . During
the long weary night many children have to be kept awake
by having cold water dashed in their faces, and when
morning comes, they throw themselves upon their beds—
often still warm from the bodies of their brothers and
sisters—without taking off their clothing. 'When I works
nights, I'se too tired to undress when I gits home, an' so I
goes to bed wif' me clo's on me,' lisped one little girl in
Augusta, Georgia."

Reverend Murphy's eloquence, articles by a handful of
newspapermen, pressure from the Alabama Child Labor
Committee—all helped convince the governors of both
Georgia and Alabama to take a stand against child labor.
In 1901, the first child labor bills were introduced in four
states in the South. The legislatures of the four leading
textile states—North Carolina, South Carolina, Alabama
and Georgia—were asked to pass laws that would curb
industry's right to exploit children.

State labor unions supported the bills as well. Union
members realized that jobs given to children were taken
from them. Though many workers were concerned with
the harm being done to the children, most union pressure
to end child labor came from workers who realized that
children could take their jobs away . . . unless. Unless the
government put a stop to child labor.

Naturally, industrialists opposed these bills. Not only
because they stood to lose an important source of cheap
labor. But because they, too, felt moral issues were
involved. But their moral issues were quite different from
Reverend Murphy's. The capitalists questioned whether any

person or government had the right to tell them how to run their business. After all, this is a free country, they reasoned. Anyone who tells me whom I can hire, for how many hours, at how much pay is just robbing me of some of my freedom. And *that's* immoral, the capitalists insisted.

Would the government dare to try to control business? The reformers insisted that it must. Without government control, stored up human misery would some day explode, possibly in revolution. Already there had been strikes in

several industries. Wouldn't it be wiser to take a fair profit and give a fair wage?

Cool, sane voices were asking for some government control to limit the power of big business. Cool, sane voices were asking for a compromise between the forces of labor and capital. It took some time, but little by little more and more people began to listen. Still, the reformers had a long way to go.

In 1901, their proposed bills were not passed by the four

Girl factory workers in the door way of a cotton mill (about 1890)

southern state legislatures. But reformers are not easily discouraged. It is almost impossible for them to conceive of defeat. There are setbacks, but not failures. Their forces grew and they worked even harder. In 1903, five southern states passed laws setting fourteen as a minimum age for children working in factories.

At least, it was a beginning.

While the South was trying to get its first child labor laws passed, northern states were trying to improve theirs. One of the biggest problems, the northern states discovered, was seeing that the laws were actually enforced once they were passed. Government inspectors were supposed to check up on whether or not industries were obey-

Boys stoking furnaces in a glass factory (1905)

ing the law. But according to labor historian Elizabeth Brandeis, "in the spring of 1902, the trade unions, the New Jersey Consumers League, the State Charities Aid Association, and the press attacked the employment of underage children and the negligence of inspectors. Boy labor in the glass factories was the object of greatest complaint. The agitation in New York also arose largely from failures to enforce the law."

New Yorkers who had fought for child labor legislation learned that legislation was only half the battle won. The other half was to ensure that the laws would be enforced.

Robert Hunter, whose writing did so much to expose the evils of child labor, was at that time head worker of

the University Settlement of New York City. He formed a group consisting of Florence Kelley, formerly of Hull House and now secretary of the National Consumers' League, Felix Adler, professor of social ethics at Columbia, and V. Everett Macy, philanthropist and banker. They called their organization the New York Child Labor Committee.

Some idea of the huge influence the New York Child Labor Committee had on public opinion and legislation can be gathered from a letter sent to Robert Hunter in 1903. It came from the congressman who introduced several child labor bills in the New York legislature:

"At the outset I found it to be the almost universal opinion held by members of the Legislature that the legislation was too advanced, and would never be enacted into law. That the contrary result was obtained, was due solely to the magnificent campaign waged by you. So thoroughly was the work done that all opposition was silenced through fear of opposing the intelligent public opinion that had been aroused."

Robert Hunter, Jane Addams, Reverend Murphy, Florence Kelley—their voices were getting louder and louder. There was definitely a rising interest in the topic of child labor. In the four years between 1897 and 1901, there were four articles on the topic of the working child published in America. In the four years between 1902 and 1906, sixty-nine articles were published.

Still, the leading figures in each state felt frustrated at every turn. Perhaps, they thought, a national organization would have more strength.

In the spring of 1904, they met in New York and formed the National Child Labor Committee. Professor Felix Adler served without salary as president of the committee and Samuel McCune, another professor of sociology, acted as secretary. The only salaried workers were two ministers, A. J. McKelway and Owen R. Lovejoy, who worked for the committee full time and a little bit more.

Eventually, cooperation came from many sources. The National Consumers' League, the General Federation of Women's Clubs, the American Federation of Labor. By 1910, twenty-two states were working with the National Child Labor Committee.

United and well-organized, with an extraordinary leadership, the National Child Labor Committee, according to a famous historian, undertook the task of abolishing child labor in the United States. Not only with moral zeal but also with a plan. It undertook investigations of conditions in various states, selecting those industries where the child labor problem appeared to be the most serious: in glass factories, textile mills, truck gardens, berry fields, canneries, street trades and night messenger service.

The committee held yearly conferences. It published the reports of its investigations. It put out a magazine called *The Child Labor Bulletin* and another called *The American Child*.

The committee agitated for reform, educated the people to want reform, studied the way to get reform.

In 1911, the committee proposed a Uniform Child Labor Law which was recommended to the states by the National Conference on Uniform State Laws. It proposed a minimum age of fourteen years for employment in manu-facturing. It asked that sixteen be made the minimum age for going down to work in the mines. It suggested a maximum work day of eight hours for children. Night work for children would be prohibited. And, in addition, industry would be forced to have legal proof of a child's age before employing him.

In 1904, not a single state in the union had passed a law covering all five of these most basic needs.

By today's standards, just fifty years later, the commit-tee's extravagant goals seem almost pitiful. Where were their demands for compulsory education? Where were their demands for safety devices and proper sanitary condi-tions to protect children's health? Why was fourteen con-sidered an acceptable age for a child to begin his working life? Was childhood actually over at fourteen? That's the year when most of today's children enter high school.

These reformers were idealists, not revolutionaries. They expected to progress step by step. Yet, even the most radical of them probably never pictured a society such as the one we live in today. Almost all American children finish high school. Half of them go on to college. Many of those go on to graduate work. Except for babysitting and summer jobs, few children go to work until they are eighteen. Many don't go to work until they've finished college, at twenty-two. Storekeepers' children, farmers' children, workingmen's children all have opportunities for education that even Robert Hunter and Jane Addams must have once believed would always belong exclusively to the rich.

Chapter Seven

THE MUCKRAKERS

In 1905, Theodore Roosevelt was elected President of the United States. In his inaugural address, the new President recommended a book to his fellow citizens. He suggested that they read Jacob Riis's *How the Other Half Lives*. It was this book, he hinted, that marked the beginning of his growing up. It was this book that helped drive him toward the presidency. He said he planned to act on what he had learned from it.

How the Other Half Lives was actually just a fraction of a huge volume of protest that Jacob Riis poured out over the years. A Danish-born immigrant, Riis's articles appeared first in the *New York Tribune* and later in the *Evening Sun*.

With John Spargo, Marie Van Vorst, Robert Hunter, Edwin Markham, Ida Tarbell, Ray Stanmard Baker and many, many others, Riis taught an entire generation how it felt to be poor.

President Roosevelt, in a speech delivered in 1906, gave

these new journalists and the religious leaders who joined with them the name which was to go down in history. "The muckrackers," he called them.

"In Bunyan's *Pilgrim's Progress*," President Theodore Roosevelt reminded the nation, "you may recall the description of the Man with the Muckrake, the man who could look no way but downward, with the muckrake in his hand, but would neither look up nor regard the crown he was offered, but continued to take to himself the filth of the floor.

"I will regard as my benefactor," the President continued, "any writer or speaker, every man who on the platform, or in book, magazine or newspaper, attacks with merciless severity, providing that he in his turn remembers that the attack is of use only if it is absolutely truthful."

With one hand, President Roosevelt was giving the muckrakers a warm pat on the back. With the other, he was suggesting that perhaps they'd better go easy. A little muck goes a long way. There was warning as well as approval in that speech.

If Theodore Roosevelt was somewhat leery that the muckrakers might make too large a wave, they were equally suspicious of him.

For one thing, he had been born into one of America's wealthiest families. For another, he had a tendency to be carried away by his own dramatics.

Teddy Roosevelt spouted moral indignation like an overwrought whale. Shaking his walking stick at unseen but ever-present enemies, he threatened, ranted, cajoled. And an entire generation of middle-class young people adored him.

Theodore Roosevelt

"The man," Teddy Roosevelt said, "who wrongly holds that every human right is secondary to his profit, must now give way to the advocate of human welfare, who rightly maintains that every man holds his property subject to the general right of the community to regulate its use to whatever degree public welfare may require it."

That sounded as though President Roosevelt believed the capitalists' insistence on their "right to freedom" was not entirely justified. The muckrakers couldn't have agreed more.

But in other speeches, Teddy Roosevelt warned about the danger of "mob rule." Just who was that mob, if not the ordinary working people of the United States, the muckrakers wondered.

Teddy Roosevelt was fiercely independent and considered himself above class loyalty. He claimed to have no

great respect for businessmen with "the money touch."
Seeing far into the future, he realized that an increasingly
powerful *national* government was necessary. Not just
state laws, but federal laws were needed to curb the social
injustices that the industrial revolution had brought with
it.

Here the President and the reformers were sometimes in
agreement. But, unfortunately, the reformers themselves
could not always agree. Some were convinced that federal
laws were, in fact, necessary to limit child labor. Others
believed progress would come sooner if each state passed
its own child labor laws.

In 1906, during Teddy Roosevelt's administration, a
national child labor bill appeared before Congress. It was
defeated. But it did not have the backing of the National
Child Labor Committee. As in all new situations, the
industrial revolution had posed new problems. It wasn't
always easy to agree on the answers.

The tremendous impact of the muckrakers was that
they didn't try to provide answers. They simply reported
what they saw. Bare, barren, hideous as the facts were,
they told them.

The rest was up to the people.

Jacob Riis, for instance, did not preach. He reported. He
lit up dark corners and forced people to see what filth lay
in them.

The rest was up to the people.

New laws were written because of Jacob Riis's investigations. But he didn't write the laws or tell the people how
to get them passed. He wrote the stories. The people did
the rest.

Riis's special beat was the Lower East Side of Manhattan. His special story—urban poverty. Here, in downtown Manhattan, Italian immigrants were crowded together in "Little Italy," bounded by Mott Street to the east and Mulberry to the west. Chinese lived in Chinatown. Jewish immigrants had a few square blocks of crumbling tenements Riis called "Jewtown." Russian immigrants, Polish, Bohemian—each had their own wretched ghetto. They competed furiously with each other for the chance to make a bit of money and get out. Street gang wars were a commonplace occurrence. If a Pole, Russian, Italian or other "foreigner" appeared in a neighborhood other than his own, the local gang let him know he was on foreign territory. Crime flourished in these crowded tenements as men became more desperate.

New York City, as Riis saw it, was divided in half. One half, uptown, with comfortable, secure homes of the middle and upper classes. The other half, the tenements and ghettos of the immigrant poor. His book, *How the Other Half Lives*, took his readers with him into those tenements.

Riis's description of the "sweated shop" revealed the depth of the depravity that created this system. The sweating system was used in New York, as it was in Chicago, to cut costs and increase profits. Just as they did in Chicago, factories farmed out work to a "sweater." Since the work was not being done in a factory, the manufacturer and the "sweater" could blithely ignore all government regulations designed to help the worker. In New York, just as in Chicago, there was no one to know that children under the legal age were working rather than going to school. There was no one to know that the "sweat shop" stayed open hours longer than the law permitted, or that safety and fire regulations couldn't have mattered less. No one to know— at least not until Jacob Riis began his violent attack on the "sweated" industries.

"Many harsh things have been said of the 'sweater,' that really apply to the system in which he is necessary," Riis wrote. "It can at least be said of him that he is no worse than the conditions that created him. The sweater is simply the middleman, a workman, like his fellows . . . but with the accidental possession of two or three sewing machines, or of enough credit to hire them. He drums up work among the clothing houses. Of workmen he can get enough. Every shipload from German ports brings them to his door, clamoring for work. Often there are two, sometimes three sets of sweaters on one job. They work with the rest when they are not drumming up trade, driving their 'hands' as they drive their machine, for all they are worth, and making a profit on their work. . . . The workman growls not at the hard labor, or the poor pay, but over the pennies another is coining out of his sweat, and on the first opportunity turns sweater himself, and takes revenge by driving an even harder bargain than his rival tyrant. . . .

"The bulk of the sweater's work is done in the tenements, which the law that regulates factory labor does not reach. . . . The tenement shops serve as a supplement through which the law is successfully evaded. Ten hours is the legal work day in the factories, and nine o'clock the closing hour at the latest. Forty-five minutes at least must be allowed for dinner, and children under sixteen must not be employed unless they can read and write English; none at all under fourteen. . . . In the tenement, the child works unchallenged from the day he is old enough to pull a thread. There is no such thing as a dinner hour; men, women, and children eat while they work, and the 'day' is lengthened at both ends. Factory hands take their work with them at the close of the lawful day to eke out their scanty earnings by working overtime at home. Little chance on this ground for the campaign of education that alone can bring needed relief; small wonder that there are whole settlements on this East Side where English is practically an unknown tongue, though the children are both willing and anxious to learn. 'When shall we find the time to learn?' asked one of them of me once. I owe him the answer yet. . . .

"Take the Second Avenue Elevated Railroad at Chatham Square and ride up half a mile through the sweaters district. Every open window of the big tenements, that stand like a continuous brick wall on both sides of the way, gives you a glimpse of one of these shops as the train goes speeding by. Men and women and children bending over their machines, or ironing clothes at the window, half naked. Proprieties do not count on the East Side; nothing counts that cannot be converted into hard cash. The road is like a big gangway through an endless workroom where vast multitudes are forever laboring. Morning, noon, or night it makes no difference; the scene is always the same."

And inside the tenement, "up two flights of dark stairs, three, four, with new smells of cabbage, of onions, of frying fish, on every landing, whirring sewing machines behind closed doors betraying what goes on within, to a door that opens to admit a bundle and a man. A sweater, this. Five men and a woman, two girls not yet fifteen and a boy who says unasked that he is fifteen, and lies in saying it, are at the machines sewing knickerbockers, 'knee pants' in the Ludlow Street dialect. The floor is littered ankle-deep with half-sewn garments. In the 'alcove' on a couch made up of many dozens of pants ready for the finisher, a bare-legged baby with pinched face is asleep. A fence of piled-high clothing keeps him from rolling off on the floor. The faces, hands and arms to the elbow of everyone in the room are black with the color of the cloth on which they are working. . . .

"A child works on the machine for this sweater twelve hours a day, turning out three dozen knee pants, for which he receives forty-two cents a dozen. . . . He is the oldest of four children at home. . . . His rent is twelve dollars a month; his wages for a hard week's work less than eight dollars."

That was New York's Lower East Side, the land of plenty discovered by thousands of Europeans who emigrated in the hope of finding an end to hunger at last.

"This great nation in its commercial madness devours its babies." That was how John Spargo saw America. Like Jacob Riis, John Spargo was a muckraker. He wanted the filth cleaned up. He wrote volumes of newspaper columns, magazine articles, eyewitness reports in the hope of waking a sleeping nation.

"There are more than 80,000 children employed in the

The Lower East Side, "the land of plenty"

textile industries of the United States," one of Spargo's articles informed the public, and most were "little girls. In these industries conditions are undoubtedly worse in the southern states than elsewhere, though I have witnessed many pitiable cases of child slavery in northern mills which equalled almost anything I have ever seen in the south. During the Philadelphia textile workers' strike in 1903, I saw at least a score of children ranging from eight to ten years of age who had been working in the mills prior to the strike. One little girl of nine I saw in the Kensington Labor Lyceum. She had been working for almost a year before the strike began, she said, and careful inquiry proved her story to be true. When 'Mother' Mary Jones started with her little 'army' of child toilers to march to Oyster Bay, in order that the President of the United States might see for himself some of the little ones who had actually been employed in the mills of Philadelphia, I happened to be engaged in assisting the strikers. For two days I accompanied the little 'army' on its march, and thus had an excellent opportunity of studying the children. Amongst them were several from eight to eleven years of age, and I remember one little girl who was not quite eleven telling me with pride that she had 'worked two years and never missed a day.' "

One evening, Spargo writes, he found himself "outside of a large flax mill in Paterson, New Jersey, while it disgorged its crowd of men, women, and children employees. All the afternoon, as I lingered in the tenement district near the mills, the comparative silence of the streets oppressed me. There were many babies and very small children, but the older children, whose boisterous play one expects in such streets, were wanting. 'If thow'lt bide till th' mills shut for th' day, thow'lt see plenty of 'em—big kids as plenty as small taties,' said one old woman to whom I spoke about it. She was right. At six o'clock the whistles shrieked, and the streets were suddenly filled with people, many of them mere children. Of all the crowd of tired, pallid, and languid-looking children I could only get speech with one, a little girl who claimed thirteen years, though she was smaller than many a child of ten. Indeed, as I think of her now, I doubt whether she would have come up to the standard of normal physical development either in weight or stature for a child of ten. One learns, however, not to judge the ages of working children by their physical appearance, for they are usually behind other children in height, weight, and girth of chest—often as much as two or three years. If my little Paterson friend was thirteen, perhaps the nature of her employment will explain her puny, stunted body. She works in the 'steaming room' of the flax mill. All day long, in a room filled with clouds of steam, she has to stand barefooted in pools of water twisting coils of wet hemp. When I saw her she was dripping wet, though she said that she had worn a rubber apron all day. In the coldest evenings of winter little Marie, and hundreds of other little girls, must go out from the superheated steaming rooms into the bitter cold in just that condition. No wonder that such children are stunted and underdeveloped!

"In textile mill towns like Biddeford, Maine; Manchester, New Hampshire; Fall River and Lawrence, Massachusetts, I have seen many such children, who, if they were twelve or fourteen according to their certificates and the companies' registers, were not more than ten or twelve in reality. I have watched them hurrying into and away from the mills, 'those receptacles, in too many instances, for living human skeletons, almost disrobed of intellect,' as Robert Owen's burning phrase describes them. I do not doubt that, upon the whole, conditions in the textile industries are better in the north than in the south, but they are nevertheless too bad to permit of self-righteous boasting and complacency. And in several other departments of industry conditions are no whit better in the north than in the south. The child-labor problem is not sectional, but national."

Industrialists would have liked Americans to believe that the nationwide practice of exploiting children was actually nationally advantageous. Child labor was not an outgrowth of their own greed, capitalists insisted. They were not simply serving their own ends. But, in fact, as they frequently stated, they were performing a noble act.

"The most beautiful sight that we see is the child at labor," according to Asa G. Caudler, founder of the Coca Cola Company. "As early as he may get at labor the more beautiful, the more useful does his life get to be."

For children working in the coal mines, for instance, how "beautiful" did life get to be? The census of 1900 reported that twenty-five thousand boys under sixteen worked in mines and quarries. There was more child labor in the coal-mining state of Pennsylvania than in any other state in the Union.

John Spargo went down into the mines with the children, returned with them to their homes at night, ate their food and lived their lives. And of one thing he became certain. He couldn't live their lives for long and survive.

"In the state of Pennsylvania," he wrote, "there are thousands of little 'breaker boys' employed, many of them not more than nine or ten years old. The law forbids the employment of children under fourteen, and the records of the mines generally show that the law is 'obeyed.' Yet in May, 1905, an investigation by the National Child Labor Committee showed that in one small borough of 7,000 population, among the boys employed in breakers thirty-five were nine years old, forty were ten, forty-five were eleven, and forty-five were twelve—over one hundred and fifty boys illegally employed in one section of boy labor in one small town! . . .

"Work in the coal breakers is exceedingly hard and dangerous. Crouched over the chutes, the boys sit hour after hour, picking out the pieces of slate and other refuse from the coal as it rushes past to the washers. From the cramped position they have to assume, most of them become more or less deformed and bent-backed like old men. When a boy has been working for some time and begins to get round-shouldered, his fellows say that 'He's got his boy to carry round wherever he goes.' The coal is hard, and accidents to the hands, such as cut, broken, or crushed fingers, are common among the boys. Sometimes there is a worse accident: a terrified shriek is heard, and a boy is mangled and torn in the machinery, or disappears in the chute to be picked out later smothered and dead. Clouds of dust fill the breakers and are inhaled by the boys, laying the foundations for asthma and miners' consumption. I once stood in a breaker for half an hour and tried to do the work a twelve-year-old boy was doing day after day, for ten hours at a stretch, for sixty cents a day. The gloom of the breaker appalled me. Outside the sun shone brightly, the air was pellucid, and the birds sang in chorus with the trees and the rivers. Within the breaker there was blackness, clouds of deadly dust enfolded everything, the harsh, grinding roar of the machinery and the ceaseless rushing of coal through the chutes filled the ears. I tried to pick out the pieces of slate from the hurrying stream of coal, often missing them; my hands were bruised

and cut in a few minutes; I was covered from head to foot with coal dust, and for many hours afterwards I was expectorating some of the small particles of anthracite I had swallowed.

"I could not do that work and live, but there were boys of ten and twelve years of age doing it for fifty and sixty cents a day. Some of them had never been inside of a school; few of them could read a child's primer. True, some of them attended the night schools, but after work-

Young coal miners from Gary, Indiana (Lewis W. Hine, 1908, George East-man House Collection)

ing ten hours in the breaker the educational results from attending school were practically nil. 'We goes fer a good time, an' we keeps de guys wots dere hoppin' all de time," said little Owen Jones, whose work I had been trying to do. How strange that barbaric patois sounded to me as I remembered the rich, musical language I had so often heard other little Owen Joneses speak in faraway Wales. As I stood in that breaker I thought of the reply of the small boy to Robert Owen. Visiting an English coal mine one day, Owen asked a twelve-year-old lad if he knew God. The boy stared vacantly at his questioner: 'God?' he said, 'God? No, I don't. He must work in some other mine.' "

Another writer, reporting in *The Labor Standard*, gave his eyewitness story on the breaker room of a Pennsylvania colliery.

"In a little room in this big, black shed—a room not twenty feet square—forty boys are picking their lives away. The floor of the room is an inclined plane, and a stream of coal pours constantly in. They work here, in this little black hole, all day and every day, trying to keep cool in summer, trying to keep warm in winter, picking away among the black coals, bending over till their little spines are curved, never saying a word all the livelong day. These little fellows go to work in this cold dreary room at seven o'clock in the morning and work till it is too dark to see any longer. For this they get one dollar to three dollars a week. Not three boys in this roomful could read or write. Shut in from everything that is pleasant, with no chance to learn, with no knowledge of what is going on about them, with nothing to do but work, grinding their little lives away in this dusty room, they are no more than the wire screens that separate the great lumps of coal from the small. They had no games; when their day's work is done they are too tired for that. They know nothing but the difference between slate and coal."

But there was hope for the breaker boys. If they lived, they would eventually graduate to the mine depths. They might even become door tenders, switch boys or mule drivers. There was only one catch. Down in the pits, the work was harder, the danger greater.

"Here, far below the surface," Spargo wrote, "the boys assume the same risks as the men, and are surrounded by the same perils. Nor is it in Pennsylvania only that these conditions exist. In the bituminous mines of West Virginia, boys of nine or ten are frequently employed. I met one little fellow ten years old in Mt. Carbon, West Virginia, last year, who was employed as a 'trap boy.' Think of what it means to be a trap boy at ten years of age. It means to sit alone in a dark mine passage hour after hour, with no human soul near; to see no living creature except the mules as they pass with their loads, or a rat or two seeking to share one's meal; to stand in water or mud that covers the ankles, chilled to the marrow by the cold draughts that rush in when you open the trap-door for the mules to pass through; to work for fourteen hours—waiting—opening and shutting a door—then waiting again— for sixty cents; to reach the surface when all is wrapped in the mantle of night, and to fall to the earth exhausted and have to be carried away to the nearest 'shack' to be revived before it is possible to walk to the farther shack called 'home.'

"Boys twelve years of age may be *legally* employed in

the mines of West Virginia, by day or by night, and for as many hours as the employers care to make them toil or their bodies will stand the strain. Where the disregard of child life is such that this may be done openly and with legal sanction, it is easy to believe what miners have again and again told me—that there are hundreds of little boys of nine and ten years of age employed in the coal mines of this state."

At first, the American people found these stories too incredible to believe. They really couldn't bear to think that such horror existed in their own land, under their own noses. It was more comfortable to think of the muck-rakers as fanatics. Or obsessed. "Look for dirt and you'll find it," was how people shrugged off the whole business.

But, inevitably, the evidence mounted. Editors kept right on publishing articles. Poets, novelists, historians, lawyers, economists joined in common cause with the muckrakers to expose the seamy side of big business. And this exposure changed the course of American history.

What could no longer be denied had to be changed. Journalism has probably never served the nation better.

Novelists, poets, story tellers of the period often did their best writing on their muckraking pieces. Possibly it was the intensity of their feelings. They were no longer asking for sympathy for the lower classes. Their voices rang with a kind of ruthless honesty. They demanded to be heard.

Edwin Markham is no longer considered a first-rate poet. Perhaps he never was. But schoolchildren were once duti-fully ordered to memorize at least two stanzas of "The Man with the Hoe."

Kids today would probably find the poem impossibly corny. But can they remain unmoved by the factual prose of his muckraking writing?

Poet Edwin Markham wrote this report about the night-working mill children. He met Helen Sisrack, eleven years old, employed at the Cambria silk mills in Dunmore, Pennsylvania, "beginning at half-past six in the evening and staying till half-past six in the morning. Haggard, hungry and faint after the night's work shifting and cleaning the bobbins, this child had an hour's walk in the chill of the morning over the lonesome fields to her home.

AN AWFUL BLOT.

"What did the mill-baron give this girl for her pitiful effort? Three cents an hour! Three cents she got for her surrender of sleep and strength, play and study. . . ."

Markham showed how employers got around the meager minimum age laws:

"A large part of the work in a silk mill is done in a warm, moist atmosphere, out of which the night workers must plunge into the rawness of the early morning. At the edge of day we may see one flood of little workers pouring out and another pouring in. And the ingoing children look as weary as the outgoing ones; all are worn, haggard, and unrested. Sometimes the night-children are held overtime to get in their ends, while little day-workers wait outside, hugging the walls in the biting cold till there is place for them at the frames.

"If we ask any one of these little creatures how old he (or she) is, none is small enough to be taken unawares. All are above thirteen. But their mathematics are sadly tangled when one questions them further.

" 'How old are you?' was asked of one of these spinners.

" 'Fourteen,' she promptly answered.

" 'How long have you been working in the mill?'

" 'Three years and a half.'

" 'How old were you when you began?'

" 'Thirteen.'

"Between the lines of this staccato dialogue one may see the easy mill-town custom of sliding the age-scale to fit the words of the law. . . .

"Inside the mill," Markham reported, "there is the constant strain of young muscle matched against untiring machinery. The children at the frames must stand all night, always alert, always watchful for broken threads, nimble to let no loose end be caught in with other threads. Nor .must any loose curls or dangling braids adorn the heads of the little mill-folk. Braids and curls are for the picture-book children; or for the little misses who wear the silk, not for the little workers who spin the silk. Childish things must be put aside by our army of wage-earning children.

"Reverend Peter Roberts, for years a resident of the anthracite regions, states that he has seen little girls before the silk frames, their short skirts tied close with string, so that they should not catch in the wheels and drag the child into the jaws of the machine. Frequently boys and girls have to stand on a stool to reach their work; although it is said that sometimes in the South frames are obligingly made of kindergarten size to accommodate the mill-mites."

Markham made the public aware of a report that probably would have been overlooked without him. "The Minnesota Bureau of Labor finds that in hundreds of cases children of the laboring classes are hired to tend intricate machinery which the children of the sheltered classes would no more be allowed to approach alone than they would be allowed to approach the snarling tiger of the circus."

Another of Markham's pieces told of an account: "A Philadelphia paper contained (December, 1906) the story of a little girl who worked for three dollars a week in a woolen mill in that city. The floors of woolen mills are always slippery with wool-grease. The child slipped, and thrusting out her arm she was caught in the cogs of an unguarded machine. Her right arm was broken in seven places from wrist to shoulder. No automobile was called, as would have been the case if little Edytha Vere de Vere were to have slipped and hurt her poor head. Instead, the child walked nearly a mile to the nearest hospital. Her arm was so jaggedly chopped up that it didn't mend straight, and she is a cripple for life. But like the children blinded by splintering glass or the children struck by flying shuttles or the children mangled in rushing coal chutes or the children unfingered in speeding box factories—like all these, this girl, this little martyr of labor, goes to fill up that black page of statistics that records the fact that, among wage-earners, the boys under sixteen have twice as many accidents as the men, while the girls under sixteen have three times as many accidents as the women."

That was certainly not Edwin Markham's most poetic writing. Except that its major concern was justice. And isn't justice really poetry after all?

An amazing variety of people turned to raking muck. One of the most influential was a gentlewoman one would expect to find at home, pouring tea. Instead, Marie Von Vorst went out into the mills and worked alongside the poor young girls who were doomed to stay in them for life. But did mill work have to be such a dreadful fate? Was there any real reason why mills should be grim as jails? No reason at all, if the owner were willing to make a reasonable profit.

In a knitting mill, Marie Von Vorst discovered that " 'spooling' is hard on the left arm and the side. Heart disease is a frequent complaint amongst spoolers," who included "more children than young girls, more young girls than women."

Of all the angry voices raised in that first decade of the

twentieth century, none was more influential than Robert Hunter's. Nor more angry. And surely no one was more original.

"The nation," he wrote, "is engaged in a traffic for the labor of children. By the introduction of the little ones into mines, factories and mills, we do a direct evil for which we are definitely responsible. . . . At this moment . . . over 1,700,000 children under fifteen years of age are toiling in fields, factories, mines and workshops.

"Child labor," Hunter held, "is synonymous with child slavery." It had nothing in common, he maintained, with the old-fashioned home workshops. "Compare them with the prison-like factory of today, with great chimneys, and huge volumes of smoke blackening the sky, the walls trembling with the ceaseless regular throbs of great and intricate machines, the maze of pulleys, cogs, the humid, artificial air, the odor of perspiration, the yelling of one operative to another, which the din of steel jamming steel makes it impossible to hear, the alert, strained look of the working children, rushing from one machine to another, from lever to roll, back and forth, hour after hour for ten or twelve hours, day after day from year's end to year's end."

That may be a prize-winning run-on sentence, but it does say it.

Robert Hunter didn't simply condemn child labor; he attempted to analyze its causes and predicted its end amazingly accurately.

"For several reasons child labor has become an evil. From a national point of view it is a waste of the nation's most valuable asset—manhood. From an industrial point of view it would, if unrestricted, exhaust the industrial resources of the working people. Instead of being a way to develop a strong and powerful working class, capable and efficient in industry, it is the one most effective way of weakening and rendering impotent the work forces, of undermining their capacity, and of producing an inert, inefficient mass of laborers. To the child it is ruinous. . . .

"These injuries which child labor inflicts upon the children are terrible; but they are, perhaps, no more important than the injuries child labor inflicts on society. As a matter of fact, child labor often retards industrial progress. Through cheap labor, manufacturers are often able to retain and perpetuate methods of manufacture which are unnecessary and antiquated. The so-called belated industries, like the sweating system, are made possible only through the cheapness of child and woman labor. Greed for profits alone makes it necessary for children of six years to carry the newly blown glass bottles from hot ovens to a place for cooling. The same thing can be done by mechanical means. Mechanical ingenuity and inventive skill are enabled to lie dormant because the labor of children and women is cheap and plentiful. Mrs. Sidney Webb of England gives this illustrative fact, 'When the employers in the woollen manufacture found themselves debarred from the employment of children, they invented the piecing machine.' And Professor Franklin H. Giddings speaks even more broadly when he says: 'Modern civilization does not require, it does not need, the drudgery of needlewomen or the crushing toil of men in a score of life-destroying occupations. If these wretched beings should drop out of existence and no others stood ready to fill their places, the economic activities of the world would not greatly suffer. A thousand devices latent in inventive brains would quickly make good any momentary loss.'

"Another evil of economic importance results from the well-known fact that the labor of children is constantly in competition with the labor of their elders. In most cases it means that the child displaces the adult.

"This destruction of the little ones, now so unnecessary and so obvious, is a kind of cannibalism. We no longer eat each other, but there can be no question that some of us live, and even win our pleasures and luxuries, by the ruin of others.

"But if we are to use the word 'cannibal' in this new sense, let us begin by applying it to those employers, in the parasitic industries, who go to our legislative halls in order to defeat child-labor laws, using the argument that only by the toil of infants are they enabled to make profits. Is it possible that this is saying too much?"

There is no doubt that Robert Hunter was not only a man of conscience and courage, but a brilliant economist as well. In 1904, he predicted "that the United States will dominate, in the near future, the commerce of the world. There will be few to question the important contribution which the working people of the United States have made to this marvellous industrial growth which enables us to take a prominent place in the world-wide commerce. This position of power is due to the superior ability and intelligence of American labor; in order to maintain it, we must as carefully guard the quality, ability, intelligence, and efficiency of labor as we now guard the security of capital."

In other words, let's not waste our youth. Let's get the

young people out of the mills and into the schools. That's where they belong. That is, if America wants an educated, intelligent working class to make it the most powerful nation in the world.

Just how great an influence did the muckrakers have on the American people? Their articles appeared in *Hampton's, Collier's, Cosmopolitan, Pearson's, McClure's* and the *Arena.* These were the most popular, least expensive magazines of the time. They were not high-flown literary periodicals. They were what radio and television are to Americans today. Picture speaker after speaker getting up before TV cameras and blasting away at the corruption in American society. Imagine eloquent, fiery attacks on the inadequacy of poverty programs, on government spending or on American military bases in foreign lands. Would the viewers be upset? Would their actions be affected by what they saw and heard? Would there be discussion, excitement, protest? And as a result, progress? It's very likely.

The period of the muckrakers' greatest influence lasted approximately ten years. Jacob Riis's *How the Other Half Lives* was published in 1890. By 1900, the movement was in full bloom. The last of the great muckraking magazines, *Hampton's,* went out of business in 1911.

Those were ten exciting years. And proud years, too. After reading the muckrakers, it might seem logical to ask, "Proud of what?" Why, proud of the muckrakers, of course. And of the editors who gave them the freedom to write what they saw. And of the publishers who risked printing their controversial articles. And of the public, who read these articles. And cared.

The muckrakers couldn't kill child labor. But they did

Jacob Riis

hit it hard. They made it hard for the comfortable classes to ignore such brutality simply because they couldn't see it. They made it hard for the government to ignore what was going on in the land of "freedom" and "democracy." And they gave the very poor, who were the victims of the system, the support they needed.

Sometimes people are so beaten down by misery they actually begin to believe misery is all they deserve. They feel resigned instead of angry. The child laborers and their parents were often far too resigned. There were the rich and there were the poor, they reasoned. The rich were powerful. The poor were not. What could poor people do except live out each day? Work to buy bread? They had given up asking "Why?" The muckrakers asked for them. And the answer came out the same each time. The children of the poor worked to make rich men richer.

The rich were powerful. The poor were not. But the poor were many. And that, they came to understand, was another kind of power.

Chapter Eight

THE CHILDREN STRIKE

I t took time for men to realize that no matter how
weak they were when they
stood alone, together they were strong.

In the early days of the industrial revolution, artisans
often joined crafts or guilds. Later on some of these guilds
grew into the first trade unions.

In the 1880's an organization called the Knights of
Labor tried to organize workingmen to fight in their own
cause. The Knights of Labor were particularly aware of
child labor. At the time of the Knights of Labor's greatest
influence, from 1880 to 1890, many states passed bills
regulating child labor.

In the five years from 1885 to 1889, ten states that had
no child labor laws before passed bills fixing a minimum
age at which children could work. And six new states set
a limit on the number of hours that children could do
night work.

But during the 1890's the Knights of Labor lost much of
its popularity. Workers began to join a new union called

the American Federation of Labor. The A. F. of L. was concerned with the rights of working people, but not particularly with protecting child workers.

Most early attempts of labor unions to bargain with management failed. Few of the early strikes succeeded in accomplishing much, if anything, for labor, either. Very often, in fact, strikes set the workers back.

The workers hoped to injure industrialists by shutting down their factories and cutting off their profits. Instead, the workers were often the losers. They didn't have enough money to hold out for long. The industrialists did. When the workers tried to come back to their jobs, foremen generally wouldn't take the strike leaders back. Sometimes, workers were forced to go back for even less money than they'd earned before. To teach them a lesson. Sometimes, picketing strikers were beaten by thugs hired by the industrialists. To teach them a lesson.

And many workers learned their lesson. They were afraid. Afraid to join a union, afraid to strike, afraid to be beaten, afraid of starving. And why not?

No wonder then, that it was not from the ranks of labor that the first groups of fighters for social justice rose.

There were the settlement house workers and the social workers.

There were the muckrakers.

And there were the preachers of the Social Gospel. They wondered how men could claim to live by the Bible, while they broke all its laws. The Reverend Washington Gladden and the Reverend Walter Rauschenbusch could see that "good works" and "kind ladies" could not create a heaven on this earth without help. Just as today religious leaders are up front in the fight for racial equality, a handful of ministers in the 1900's preached social equality. They called it the Social Gospel.

In 1902, Dr. Gladden wrote, "The Christian law is meant to live by, to do business by, to rule politics." A society governed by Christian ethics, Dr. Gladden predicted, would banish "rotten politics and grinding monopolies would shrivel and disappear; under its banner light and beauty, peace and plenty, joy and gladness would be let in.

"There is a certain important work to be done which no voluntary organization can succeed in doing," Dr. Gladden wrote, "a work which requires the exercise of the power of the state."

Rev. Rauschenbusch made the position of the leaders of the Social Gospel even more clear.

He would review for audiences how in the period following the Civil War, America had grown into a great nation. Settlers had cultivated the vast plains between the Mississippi River and California. The country was crisscrossed with a quarter of a million miles of railroad. Between 1870 and 1900, the number of farms doubled, and America produced almost three times as much wheat, cotton and corn as she had before. The production of coal increased 5 times, of oil 12 times and of steel 140 times. The population of the cities grew from nine million people to thirty million.

An enormous amount of energy went into this breakneck-speed expansion. But at what a cost. Farmers and laborers received pathetically little in return for their work. The cities that grew with industry were full of ugly, crowded slums. More and more, they were being governed by corrupt politicians. The human needs of the people had been neglected in the headlong rush toward physical expansion. And men and women of good will were concerned. They doubted that the future would take care of itself. The nation, they felt, needed to be aroused to its danger.

As industry grew, so did the city slums

The people themselves must take action.

"If the banner of the Kingdom of God is to enter through the gates of the future, it will have to be carried by tramping hosts of labor," Rev. Rauschenbusch predicted.

And he was right. The struggle begun by the social workers and muckrakers, carried forward by the preachers of the Social Gospel, in the end had to be fought out by the working people themselves.

In the mills of Lawrence, Massachusetts; Paterson, New Jersey; Augusta, Georgia; New York City; Philadelphia, Pennsylvania; Manchester, New Hampshire and in Biddeford, Maine, mill hands looked for an answer.

In desperation, the people of Lawrence chose what seemed the only road. Thousands of workers were employed in the towering giant that was the Wood Mill, built in Lawrence, Massachusetts, in 1905.

A vast, U-shaped building, it spread over thirty acres, employed one hundred thousand men, women and children, and produced more cloth than any other factory in the world. Both the mill and the land adjacent to it belonged to the American Woolen Company, so that almost the entire town of Lawrence was the property of the company. It built and owned the miserable tenements that housed the workers. The rents were not cheap.

As the company expanded, its need for cheap labor became more insatiable.

People everywhere were beginning to hear of Lawrence. In 1911, a city survey showed that the milk supply was perilously contaminated, and the tenements that housed the workers were described as nightmares of "darkness and dampness and dirt; dirt and discomfort and disease; death."

A committee of mill hands decided to go to Mr. Wood, president of the American Woolen Company. Perhaps his overseers kept from him the truth about their wretched lives.

Politely, they were told, "Send a letter. Address it to Mr. Wood, Lawrence. It will get there."

The letter was sent. There was no answer.

And so, the people of Lawrence found their own answer.

On the morning of January 12, 1912, quietly putting aside their work, they left the mills. The bells in the steeple on top of City Hall tolled calamitously. Twenty-five thousand men, women and children were out on strike. The wheels stopped turning. The largest mills in the world stood empty and silent.

It was bitter cold that morning. Chill, wet winds whipped at their ragged clothes as the mill workers tried to set up picket lines around the factories. The children, who possibly did not even know they were children, joined the lines. Suddenly, they were struck with a terrible rushing force of cold wetness. They ran from it, fleeing in every direction. They still didn't realize what had hit them. The mill owners had turned powerful fire hoses of icy water on the forming picket lines.

So that was the way it was going to be. There would be no talks, no compromises, no meetings between leaders of the two groups. Meetings where men of reason and good will would try to find a peaceful way out of their dilemma. Instead, it was to be a battle, each group becoming more entrenched in its determination to hold out. Win, and never mind the cost.

The mill owners counted hunger their most powerful ally. How long could people already half-starved last without food?

The workers counted greed their most powerful ally. How long could rich men watch their mills stand idle as profits poured down the drain?

Quite a long time, it turned out. Long enough for the strike at Lawrence to go down in history.

As the weeks went by, parents began to fear for their children. How many months since they'd tasted meat? Or milk? Or a bit of cheese and bread? How long had hunger lain coiled in their stomachs, a worm gnawing at their innards? And now there was this fear of violence.

A committee was formed to find homes in other cities for some of these children, where they would be cared for until the strike was over. On the day a group of children were to leave Lawrence, Colonel Sweetser, commander of the troops called in by the mill owners to "keep order," declared, "I will not permit the shipping off of little children."

"Police, acting under orders of the city marshal, clubbed, choked and knocked down the women and children," according to a news report in the *Boston Common*.

The New York Herald headline read, "Bar Shipment of Strike Children; Women Clubbed. Youngsters Trampled In Riot When Lawrence Police Halt Exportation."

Now, was there anyone in this land who still had not heard of Lawrence?

Americans everywhere spoke up.

Professor Vida Scudder of Wellesley wrote: "I would rather never again wear a thread of woolen than know my garments had been woven at the cost of such misery as I have seen."

The famous journalist, William Allen White, protested: "There was no excuse for the violence by the police."

William Dean Howells called the police action an "outrage." Could anyone think it was anything else?

Frederick W. Lehmann, legal advisor to President Taft and Chairman of the American Bar Association, declared the act "in violation of Constitutional rights."

But neither the workers nor the mill owners had counted on the determination of the other side.

The strike in Lawrence, Massachusetts, lasted sixty-three days.

On March 14, when twenty-five thousand men, women and children returned to work, they stood strong in their victory.

The owners were forced to promise two cents an hour increase to some, one cent and one cent and a half to others. They promised not to discriminate against any group in hiring and not to penalize the strike leaders.

Their promise came too late for many. They had already been penalized. The battle in Lawrence was not bloodless. A young woman was shot. A child was bayoneted in the picketing. The militia was called in and two strike leaders were jailed, eight others arrested, on charges of attempting to dynamite locations in Lawrence.

William M. Wood, the president of the American

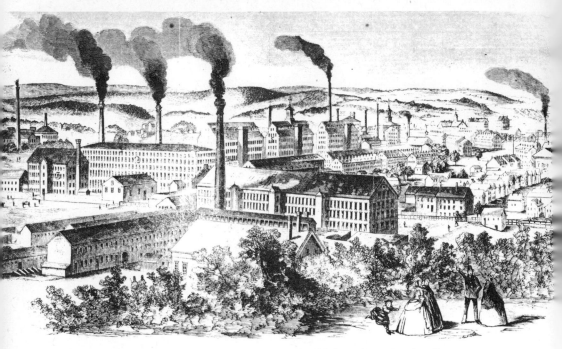

Lawrence, Massachusetts, site of the 1912 mill workers' strike

Woolen Company, was indicted on suspicion of having been involved in a dynamite plot. Both he and the labor leaders were later found innocent and released. A friend of Wood's, the man who built the Wood Mill, confessed to the crime and committed suicide.

Congressman William B. Wilson of Pennsylvania, Senator William Borah, Senator Miles Poindexter and Congressman Victor Berger all called for an investigation into the facts.

On March 2, 1912, the Committee On Rules of the House of Representatives met in Washington to look into the situation.

Congressman Berger submitted to the committee a

telegram he had received from the workers at Lawrence. It read:

DEMANDS FOR INVESTIGATION

Lawrence, Mass., February 24, 1912

Twenty-five thousand striking textile workers and citizens of Lawrence protest against the hideous brutality with which the police handled the women and children of Lawrence this morning. Carrying out the illegal and original orders of the city marshal to prevent free citizens from sending their children out of the city, striking men were knocked down, women and mothers who were trying to protect their children from the onslaught of the police were choked and clubbed.

We demand a congressional investigation before the mill owners succeed in perverting the law courts and all the forces of government and make their crying outrages the admitted law of the land.

THE STRIKERS' COMMITTEE

Congressman Berger went on to give the legal reasons for the government's investigation: "The American Woolen Company has for years been the recipient of a Government subsidy in the form of a high tariff. The claim has been made that this high tariff is levied in order to protect labor. Yet in spite of this claim it is generally conceded that these operatives are among the lowest paid of those of any industry in America. It is also conceded that they are imported from sections of Europe where the standard of living is the lowest.

"It is known, moreover, that this strike takes place as a revolt against a reduction of about fifty cents per week out of a wage averaging less than six dollars per week.

"Since it is a well-known fact that the American Woolen Company practically controls the production of worsted woolens in America, I believe it is the duty of the House of Representatives, before we undertake to fix the tariff on wool and woolen and worsted goods, to investigate and make known all the facts regarding this strike and the relations thereto of the American Woolen Company.

"Inventive genius," Congressman Berger continued, "has made it possible for capital to employ women and children where formerly the work of men was necessary. It is a well-known fact that under this system the combined earnings of an entire family usually are not greater than are the earnings of the head of a family where woman and child labor is not habitual. Yet, in spite of this fact, woman and child labor is continually increasing, and no amount of legislation seems seriously to check it. Competition and greed on the one hand and competition and hunger on the other combine to increase woman and child labor. . . .

"The strike in Lawrence is a rebellion of the wage-working class against unbearable conditions. While the manufacturers are heaping up millions in surplus value abstracted from the wealth produced by these workers, the workers themselves are doomed to lives of the utmost wretchedness."

Margaret Sanger

The hearings on the strike at Lawrence, Massachusetts, before the Committee On Rules of the House of Representatives lasted a full week.

Sixteen children were brought down from Lawrence to testify.

A young woman named Margaret Sanger, who later became one of the world's leading doctors, was asked to come from New York to tell the committee what she had observed. She was questioned by Mr. Pou and others for the committee.

MR. POU: I will be obliged to you if you will just go ahead and state in your own way what took place.

MISS SANGER: Well, I helped to take the first section of children, when there was no difficulty in getting them away. We brought them to New York and gave them supper; we took them to the Labor Temple, where people were waiting to take them to their homes; there they had a supper and they were distributed, and that was all there was to that.

Mr. Pou:　How long was that before the day we have been talking about, the 24th of February, I think it was?

Miss Sanger:　I think that was two weeks.

Mr. Pou:　How many of the children were taken to New York?

Miss Sanger:　One hundred and nineteen at this time and ninety-two a week afterwards.

Mr. Pou:　Altogether that would be something over two hundred?

Miss Sanger:　Yes, sir.

Mr. Pou:　Well, you had no trouble with the police?

Miss Sanger:　No; we had no trouble.

Mr. Pou:　They had not decided to prevent the children from leaving when you took these away?

Miss Sanger:　No; not at this time.

Mr. Pou:　Did you talk with those children about their manner of living in Lawrence and about the food they got?

Miss Sanger:　Yes, sir. I am a trained nurse, and I was especially interested in the condition of the children.

Mr. Pou:　Now, as a rule, is it true that the children of the working people in Lawrence—the class we are investigating now—only got meat once a week?

Miss Sanger:　Those were the assertions of not only the children but of the parents that I interviewed.

Mr. Foster:　How long were you in Lawrence?

Miss Sanger: I was only there one night.

Mr. Foster: You arrived in Lawrence in the evening and left the next morning?

Miss Sanger: Yes.

Mr. Foster: You did not visit any of the homes of the strikers?

Miss Sanger: No. When the people brought the children to the hall the next morning to be taken away I inquired of some of the parents about the children.

Mr. Foster: You say you are a trained nurse?

Miss Sanger: Yes, sir.

Mr. Foster: And what was the physical appearance of these children that you took to New York? You know something about how they should look; were they properly nourished?

Miss Sanger: Well, the condition of those children was the most horrible that I have ever seen.

Mr. Foster: Tell the committee something about how they looked.

Miss Sanger: In the first place, there were four little children who had chicken pox that we kept there; we would not allow them to go away; and then one of the children had just gotten over chicken pox, and the father begged us to let the child come; he had one two years old and another three and a half years old, I believe, and he begged us to let those children come, because he was a widower and had no wife or anyone to take care of these children; he left them with the neighbors during the day. So I took these little children, and we isolated them on the way to New York, and when we got there they were placed under the doctor's care. All of these children were walking about there, apparently not noticing chicken pox or diphtheria; one child had diphtheria and had been walking around, and no attention paid to it at all, and had been working up to the time of the strike. Out of the one hundred and nineteen children, four of them had underwear on, and it was the most bitter weather; we had to run all the way from the hall to the station in order to keep warm; and only four had underwear.

MR. FOSTER: You say only four had underwear?

MISS SANGER: Yes.

MR. FOSTER: What was the character of their outer clothing; was it woolen?

MR. STANLEY: Were the people working in a woolen mill?

MISS SANGER: Yes, sir.

MR. STANLEY: Where they make underwear?

MISS SANGER: Yes, sir.

MR. FOSTER: How about the outer clothing?

MISS SANGER: It was almost in rags; their coats were eaten off as though they were simply worn to shreds.

MR. FOSTER: Was it woolen clothing?

MISS SANGER: No, sir; I do not think any one of them had on any woolen clothing; that is, to my knowledge.

MR. FOSTER: What was their color? Did they seem to be well nourished?

MISS SANGER: They were very much emaciated; every child there showed the effects of malnutrition, and all of them, or almost all of them, according to the doctor's certificate that night, had adenoids and enlarged tonsils.

They were all examined at the station. We had a little time in the morning, and they were examined before they left.

Mr. Foster: They all looked thin and pale?

Miss Sanger: Yes. I would like to say that when they had this supper it would bring tears to your eyes to see them grab the meat with their hands and eat it.

Mr. Foster: They ate the meat as though they really enjoyed it?

Miss Sanger: Yes; decidedly.

Mr. Foster: And you say that there were only four out of the hundred and nineteen that had any under-clothing?

Miss Sanger: Yes, sir; and it was the bitterest weather we have had this year.

Mr. Foster: And the outer clothing was ragged?

Miss Sanger: In rags. I think perhaps twenty of them had overcoats.

Mr. Foster: What kind of shoes did they have?

Miss Sanger: Almost on the ground, except some of the older girls, who had been working in the mills; they had better shoes; but the little ones, who had to depend on the others, were in a most deplorable condition.

Mr. Foster: Did they have on woolen stockings?

Miss Sanger: I do not think any of them had a bit of wool on their bodies.

Mr. Foster: And yet working in woolen mills?

Miss Sanger: Yes, sir.

The children testified, too.

A little girl named Camella Teoli was put on the witness stand. The Chairman of the Congressional Committee questioned her.

THE CHAIRMAN: Camella, how old are you?

MISS TEOLI: Fourteen years and eight months.

THE CHAIRMAN: Where do you work?

MISS TEOLI: In the woolen mill.

THE CHAIRMAN: What sort of work do you do?

MISS TEOLI: Twisting.

THE CHAIRMAN: How much do you get a week?

MISS TEOLI: $6.55.

THE CHAIRMAN: What is the smallest pay?

MISS TEOLI: $2.64.

THE CHAIRMAN: Do you have to pay anything for your drinking water?

MISS TEOLI: Yes.

THE CHAIRMAN: How much?

MISS TEOLI: Ten cents every two weeks.

THE CHAIRMAN: Have they ever held back any pay?

MISS TEOLI: One week's pay.

THE CHAIRMAN: Does your father work, and where?

MISS TEOLI: My father works in Washington at the woolen mill.

THE CHAIRMAN: How much pay does he get for a week's work?

MISS TEOLI: $7.70.

THE CHAIRMAN: Now, did you ever get hurt in the mill?

MISS TEOLI: Yes.

THE CHAIRMAN: Can you tell the committee about that—how it happened and what it was?

MISS TEOLI: Yes.

THE CHAIRMAN: Tell us about it now, in your own way.

MISS TEOLI: Well, I used to go to school, and then a man came up to my house and asked my father why I didn't go to work, so my father says, "I don't know whether she is thirteen or fourteen years old." So the man says, "You give me four dollars and I will make the papers come from the old country saying you are fourteen." So, my father gave him the four dollars, and in one month came the papers that I was fourteen. I went to work, and about two weeks got hurt in my head.

THE CHAIRMAN: Now, how did you get hurt, and where were you hurt in the head, explain that to the committee.

MISS TEOLI: I got hurt in Washington.

THE CHAIRMAN: In the Washington Mill?

MISS TEOLI: Yes, sir.

THE CHAIRMAN: What part of your head?

MISS TEOLI: My head.

THE CHAIRMAN: Well, how were you hurt?

MISS TEOLI: The machine pulled the scalp off.

THE CHAIRMAN: The machine pulled your scalp off?

MISS TEOLI: Yes, sir.

THE CHAIRMAN: How long ago was that?

MISS TEOLI: A year ago, or about a year ago.

THE CHAIRMAN: Were you in the hospital after that?

MISS TEOLI: I was in the hospital seven months.

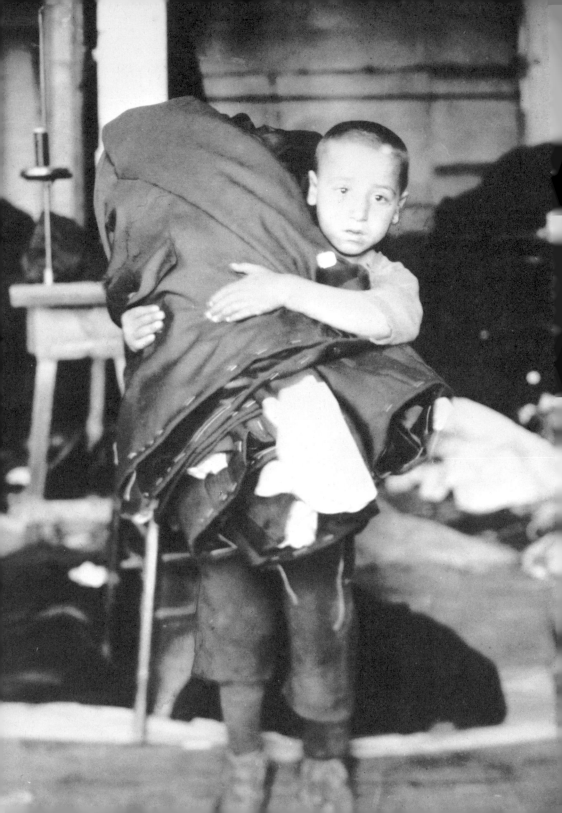

THE CHAIRMAN: Seven months?

MISS TEOLI: Yes.

MR. LENROOT: They did not pay your wages?

MISS TEOLI: No, sir.

THE CHAIRMAN: Did they arrest your father for having sent you to work at fourteen?

MISS TEOLI: Yes, sir.

THE CHAIRMAN: What did they do with him after they arrested him?

MISS TEOLI: My father told this about the man he gave four dollars to, and then they put him in again.

THE CHAIRMAN: Are you still being treated by the doctors for the scalp wound?

MISS TEOLI: Yes, sir.

THE CHAIRMAN: How much longer do they tell you you will have to be treated?

MISS TEOLI: They don't know.

THE CHAIRMAN: Are you working now?

MISS TEOLI: Yes, sir.

THE CHAIRMAN: How much are you getting?

MISS TEOLI: $6.55.

THE CHAIRMAN: How long did you go to school?

MISS TEOLI: I left when I was in the sixth grade.

THE CHAIRMAN: You left when you were in the sixth grade?

MISS TEOLI: Yes, sir.

THE CHAIRMAN: And you have been working ever since, except while you were in the hospital?

MISS TEOLI: Yes, sir.

It was easy to get papers "proving" a child was fourteen

MR. CAMPBELL: Do you know the man who came to your father and offered to get a certificate that you were fourteen years of age?

MISS TEOLI: I know the man, but I have forgot him now.

MR. CAMPBELL: You know him, but you do not remember his name now?

MISS TEOLI: Yes.

MR. CAMPBELL: Do you know what he did; what his work was?

MISS TEOLI: No.

MR. CAMPBELL: Was he connected with any of the mills?

MISS TEOLI: I don't know.

MR. CAMPBELL: Is he an Italian?

MISS TEOLI: Yes, sir.

MR. CAMPBELL: He knew your father well?

MISS TEOLI: Yes, sir.

MR. CAMPBELL: Was he a friend of your father?

MISS TEOLI: No.

MR. CAMPBELL: Did he ever come about your house visiting there?

MISS TEOLI: I don't know.

MR. CAMPBELL: I mean before he asked about your going to work in the mills?

MISS TEOLI: Yes, sir.

MR. CAMPBELL: He used to come to your house and was a friend of the family?

MISS TEOLI: Yes.

MR. CAMPBELL: You are sure he was not connected or employed by some of the mills?

MISS TEOLI: I don't know. I don't think so.

MR. CAMPBELL: Do they go around in Lawrence there and find little girls and boys in the schools under fourteen years of age and urge them to quit school and go to work in the mills?

The Committee On Rules of the House of Representatives discovered the answer. It was Yes.

Not only did factory owners urge children under the legal working age of fourteen into the mills; they were happy to accept false proof of a child's age. A nine- or ten year-old with papers to "prove" he was fourteen was "just small for his age," obviously.

More children called to testify. John Boldelar, child of immigrant parents, thought America was going to be a way out of misery.

MR. WILSON: John, about how long have you been living in this country?

MASTER BOLDELAR: Oh, about three years.

MR. WILSON: And did you go immediately to Lawrence?

MASTER BOLDELAR: Why, yes.

MR. WILSON: Are you sure about that? You went to Lawrence, you and your father both, and began working in the mill?

MASTER BOLDELAR: Yes, sir.

MR. WILSON: And have you ever lived in any other city except Lawrence?

MASTER BOLDELAR: Well, I lived in Haverhill for about half a year.

MR. WILSON: Was that before you lived in Lawrence, or after?

MASTER BOLDELAR: Well, it is after; and we moved back here again.

MR. LENROOT: John, do you remember the old country, your home over there?

MASTER BOLDELAR: Yes, sir.

MR. LENROOT: Do you remember all about it over there?

MASTER BOLDELAR: Yes, sir.

MR. LENROOT: Did you have more to eat and better times there than you did here?

MASTER BOLDELAR: Well, don't think much better. I should think I would rather have been there.

MR. LENROOT: You wish you were back?

MASTER BOLDELAR: Yes, sir.

MR. WILSON: Then, if we give you a permit to go back you will go back, will you?

MASTER BOLDELAR: I don't think I would go alone, because my father spent a lot of money for coming over here.

MR. CAMPBELL: Did you go to school?

MASTER BOLDELAR: Yes, sir.

MR. CAMPBELL: What school did you attend?

MASTER BOLDELAR: I went to Arlington school.

MR. CAMPBELL: What grade were you in when you quit?

MASTER BOLDELAR: I was in fourth grade, naval, when I quit.

MR. CAMPBELL: Were you glad when you quit school?

MASTER BOLDELAR: No, sir.

MR. CAMPBELL: You would have been glad if the law

had not permitted you to go to work until you were sixteen?

MASTER BOLDELAR: If we had had enough money I would not have quit it.

MR. CAMPBELL: But you would like to have the law changed so that boys could not go into the mill until they were sixteen?

MASTER BOLDELAR: I would; but what would we eat if I go to school? We should live on bread and water all the time?

Children working at looms in a textile factory

William Murphy testified.

THE CHAIRMAN: What is the smallest pay you get for one and a half days' work or two days' work?

MASTER MURPHY: Seventy-eight cents.

THE CHAIRMAN: Seventy-eight cents? Do you pay anything for water?

MASTER MURPHY: Five cents a week.

THE CHAIRMAN: Do they hold back a week's pay from you?

MASTER MURPHY: Yes, sir.

THE CHAIRMAN: If you are late, how about closing the doors and deducting pay?

MASTER MURPHY: If you are late two minutes, they close the door, and for seven minutes, they take off an hour's pay.

Charles Dhooghe testified.

MR. LENROOT: What do you make each week in the mill?

MASTER DHOOGHE: $4.82.

MR. LENROOT: That is what you usually make—most of the time?

MASTER DHOOGHE: Usually four dollars and a few cents.

MR. LENROOT: What is the least that you ever made there?

MASTER DHOOGHE: $1.68 for two days' work.

MR. LENROOT: Do you work most of the week nearly all the time?

MASTER DHOOGHE: No; in winter, but not in summer.

MR. LENROOT: You work pretty steadily in the winter, but not in the summer? What is the smallest pay you have got there, did you say?

MASTER DHOOGHE: $1.68.

MR. LENROOT: $1.68; yes. You are a bobbin boy now?

MASTER DHOOGHE: Yes, sir.

MR. LENROOT: What did you do before you were a bobbin boy?

MASTER DHOOGHE: Pack boy in the mule room.

MR. LENROOT: How long did you work at that?

MASTER DHOOGHE: A year and a half.

MR. LENROOT: And how much did you make there?

MASTER DHOOGHE: $6.55 for steady work.

MR. LENROOT: Why didn't you keep on that?

MASTER DHOOGHE: I could not; I was sick; the doctor told me I would have to stop. I was operated on for appendicitis.

MR. LENROOT: Was that harder work than you do now?

MASTER DHOOGHE: Yes, sir; had to work barefooted there, with only overalls and a small shirt on.

MR. LENROOT: Why did you have to do that?

MASTER DHOOGHE: You would fall; and you would have sore feet if you worked with shoes on.

MR. LENROOT: Was the water running on the floor?

MASTER DHOOGHE: Yes, sir.

Sitting in the crowded hearing room, smartly dressed in a wide-brimmed hat and a dark tailored suit, an attractive woman struggled for composure as one after another, the children were called up to testify. William Murphy, who sometimes earned seventy-eight cents a week and paid out five of them for drinking water. John Boldelar who ate meat once a week on Sundays; the other six days, only black bread and molasses. With molasses in place of butter, "we are trying to fool our stomachs," another witness said. Charles Dhooghe held up his right hand. The thumb was missing. "Cut off" in the mill, he testified.

Spectators' eyes wandered from the children to the lady in the wide-brimmed hat. "How does she feel," their glances seemed to ask, "listening to all this. Has she ever heard the like of this before?"

Mrs. Helen Taft never said. Each day, though, the wife of William Howard Taft, president of the United States, took her place in the audience and each day she listened as the nightmare unfolded.

For the children it was a holiday. Whole days away from the mill.

They stayed in warm rooms. They ate as much as they wanted. They never dreamed that life could be so rich.

And the president's wife, Mrs. Taft, had she ever dreamed that life could be so poor?

The children who came to Washington helped educate the entire nation. Even in their worst nightmares, middle-class Americans had never dreamed of lives such as these.

Now, it was up to America to educate the children. It was up to America to see that all children got what they were entitled to. Time to learn and time to play, food to eat and clothes to wear, time to sleep and time to daydream. Time to be a child and time to grow up.

Chapter Nine

LAWS WITH TEETH

I n 1916, the United States Congress passed the first federal law
regulating child labor.

The main points of the Palmer-Owen bill were:

"That it shall be unlawful for any producer, manufacturer or dealer to ship or deliver for shipment in interstate
commerce the products of any mine or quarry which have
been produced in whole or in part by the labor of children
under the age of sixteen years, or the products of any mill,
cannery, factory or manufacturing establishment which
have been produced in whole or in part by the labor of
children under the age of fourteen years of age, or by the
labor of children between the age of fourteen years and
sixteen years who work more than eight hours in any one
day or more than six days in any week, or after the hour
of seven o'clock post-meridian or before the hour of seven
o'clock ante-meridian."

What was the law actually saying?

That children had to be sixteen years or older to work
in the mines.

That children had to be fourteen years or older to do other kinds of work.

That children under sixteen could work only eight hours a day.

That children under sixteen must have a day off once a week.

That children under sixteen could not do night work.

This time the National Child Labor Committee supported the federal bill. They could see that it might take forever if each state had to pass a child labor law of its own. The American Federation of Labor, the Federal Council of Churches of Christ in America, the Farmers' Educational and Cooperative Union of America, the American Medical Association, the Democratic Party and the Republican Party were all in favor of the bill.

Almost the only people against it were the cotton mill owners in the South. Naturally, they didn't object to the sixteen-year minimum age for working in mines. It didn't affect them. But the other regulations did. They put up some strange arguments against the bill.

"The children of the South, many of them, must labor. . . ." one mill owner said. "It is a question of necessity. . . ." And he went on to add that, besides, the South would pass its own laws to protect its own children.

The only other voice heard to oppose the bill was the lawyer for the National Association of Manufacturers.

When the vote was finally taken, only two states were against the bill—North and South Carolina.

No sooner was the bill made law than a judge in North Carolina declared it unconstitutional. The Supreme Court of the United States agreed.

In 1919, another federal law, similar to the Palmer-Owen bill, was passed by Congress. The same judge in North Carolina declared it unconstitutional. Again the Supreme Court agreed with the judge from North Carolina.

Now those in favor of federal legislation tried to get an amendment regulating child labor added to our Constitution. The amendment was passed by Congress, but it was not ratified by the states.

Amazing arguments were used against the proposed amendment. It was called the "Loafer Law." Farmers were convinced that they would not be allowed to ask their children to help with farm chores. Mothers were told they'd be fined if they let their children run down to the corner store for groceries.

The Citizens' Committee to Protect Our Homes and Children put out leaflets warning that the amendment would be "a calamity to the Nation. Don't be deceived," parents were urged. "If you love your children . . . put a cross (X) opposite 'NO' on Referendum 7."

Who were these citizens on the Citizens' Committee to Protect Our Homes and Children?

Well, one was a Lowell of the Lowell Knitting Mills. Another was the former president of the Associated Industries of Massachusetts. Hardly what is generally thought of as ordinary citizens. It's hard to picture these men asking their children to help out with the farm chores. It's just as hard to picture their wives asking one of their children to run down to the corner store for a quart of milk before dinner.

Manufacturers, north and south, were afraid of the amendment. For one thing, it put the minimum working age at eighteen. They would really run out of cheap labor if they had to hire adults. And picture the taxes they would be asked to pay if every child stayed in school until he reached eighteen.

A tremendous campaign was waged against the amendment. Advertisements, leaflets, newspaper articles warned people to vote against it. Senator Stephens of Mississippi called it a "socialist movement" designed to "destroy our government."

Imagine how frightening it was to some parents when Senator Stephens declared that under the amendment "the child becomes the absolute property of the Federal Government."

No wonder American citizens, voting in 1924, refused to ratify the proposed amendment to the Constitution. They'd been scared silly by the very same industrialists who had always benefited from child labor.

If there was no hope for a federal law, reformers went back to putting pressure on the states. They directed their attention to compulsory education. Children who had to be in school, because of state education requirements, could not be in the mills or mines.

The Smith-Hughes Act was passed, promising money to states in support of their vocational schools and continuation schools. Children who left school to go to work were often required to continue their education at continuation schools. By 1932, with the promise of money for these

A boy worker in a West Virginia coal mine (Lewis Hine, 1908, George Eastman House Collection)

schools, twenty-seven states had made attendance at continuation schools compulsory. The Federal Board for Vocational Education stated that children must attend continuation school at least one hundred and forty-four days a year, during the normal waking hours. Each state was permitted to define "child" in its own way. Most states chose to consider the age of fourteen as the line between child and adult.

Those one hundred and forty-four days were one hundred and forty-four days a year children could not work.

Many people had hoped that pressure for a constitutional amendment, even though it failed, would still arouse the states' desire to limit child labor. But this did not happen. Fewer states passed child labor laws from 1923 to 1929 than in any six years in the period from 1900 to 1923.

By 1932, only half the states in the union had laws establishing what the National Child Labor Committee considered "minimum standards." These standards would require that:

1. No child under fourteen be employed.
2. No children over fourteen work more than an eight-hour day, six days a week.
3. No children do night work.
4. No children be employed in dangerous work or work that might do harm to their health or growth.
5. No child be employed without having a work permit proving his age beyond a doubt.

6. No child be employed when school is in session unless he has finished the eighth grade of elementary school.

It wasn't until 1938 that the Fair Labor Standards Act was passed by Congress. Children had been in the mills and mines for at least one hundred years. Finally, the federal government acted.

The Fair Labor Standards Act stated that no child under sixteen could work on goods that would be shipped across state lines or sent abroad. In the case of trades considered dangerous, the law required that children be at least eighteen years old.

Twelve years later, the statute was changed. This was done so that children working on farms would be protected by the federal government as well. Now it was against the law for children under sixteen to work on farms during school hours, unless they were simply helping their parents out.

At the same time, states were urged to pass laws of their own that would regulate child labor in businesses that did not have any interstate commerce. Small factories, grocery stores, newspaper deliveries do not generally do business outside their own states or even outside their own cities. It was up to the states to pass the laws that would prevent these small businessmen from abusing working children.

By 1970 all states had taken some steps toward fulfilling the minimal standards set forth by the National Child Labor Committee. In some states the laws came more slowly. It was slowest in the South.

And in many states, even when laws were passed, they were not very strong. They permitted businessmen many loopholes to get around the law.

No law is more effective than its own provisions for enforcement. A law must have teeth. It must say how someone who does not obey it will be punished. Many states passed laws without teeth. And children continued to labor.

Looking back, it's easy to see that child labor legislation has made very slow progress.

Children's work should be schoolwork. For them to do any other work is an obvious wrong. A great many people have seen that. And a great many have acted on what they have seen. There has been more humanitarian protest against the employment of children than against any other abuse in the history of labor. And still progress has been so slow.

Could it possibly be because children cannot fight their own battles and win against adults?

Chapter Ten

THE FORGOTTEN CHILDREN

Today, America has both state and federal laws to regulate child labor. But all the laws combined are not as powerful as one simple fact. We are rich. America is now the richest country in the world.

We are living in what is known as an "affluent society." Unions have grown strong and won high wages for workers. Factories work full time. Their highly paid employees can afford to buy what they themselves produce. Workers own houses and cars, dishwashers and TV's. They don't need to send their children out to work. And they don't.

America exports a great many manufactured, mass-produced items. Unfortunately, many of them are war weapons. Other nations make good customers for these. So does our own government. That means there are good foreign markets for our products and good domestic markets for our products.

Also, our industrialists have finally learned that cheap labor doesn't pay. Poor people have no money to buy goods.

With America's rich natural resources, large labor force and competitive spirit, it's natural that it became the richest nation in the world.

It's also natural that American children became the richest children in the world.

What has our affluence done for our children? They are the best fed, best housed, best dressed children in the world. They have the most toys and the most time to use them. At least seven million of them go to college. Even more finish high school. Their childhoods are the longest in the world. They have all the time they need to grow up in now.

That's why it is even more tragic that for one group of children, nothing has changed. Life is as grim, as ugly and as dangerous for them as it was for the working children in the middle of the nineteenth century. They live today as others did one hundred years ago. For them, the date could be 1870.

Who are these children?

They are the children of America's migrant workers.

Who are the migrant workers?

They are the starving Americans who live in shacks and tarpaper huts at the edges of fields. They harvest the crops we eat. They pick the fruit and berries, the lettuce and beets, the good, nourishing food Americans grow fat on. While the rest of the country diets, the migrant workers are starving to death.

In the summer, they may be in California, picking lettuce and olives and fruit. In the winter, they move on to the orange groves of Florida or the fields of Texas.

In the fall, many of these families migrate north to New

Jersey and Long Island, where the potato crop needs harvesting.

Laws that protect other workers simply don't protect the migrant workers. They move too much. Since they don't belong to any state in particular, they don't get a chance to vote. Poor and uneducated as they are, they don't even realize the power of their vote. Like the mill families of the 1800's, they are far too depressed and sunk into their misery to realize that there is a way out.

Wherever migrant farmers work, their children work alongside them. A survey made of migrant families showed that men average about thirty-two dollars a week, during the weeks they work. But their wives and children together average about forty-eight dollars. Since there are long stretches when there is no work at all, anyone can see that all hands had better pitch in when there is work to be done. Still, the migrant family rarely makes more than fifteen hundred dollars in a year.

Moving as he does from place to place, the migrant child laborer has almost no hope of ever getting out of his miserable world. He doesn't stay long enough in any one place to get even the most basic education. He may attend a local school when there's no farm work to be done. But he can't even stay long enough to figure out what the class is doing. The teacher, knowing he's about to leave soon, often neglects him. Without education, the migrant child can't hope to escape. Few of them go beyond fourth grade. Many cannot read or write.

Inspectors from the Department of Labor report that there are somewhere between one hundred thousand and six hundred thousand migrant child laborers. That's a pretty big spread, from one hundred thousand to six hundred thousand. But inspectors explain it by revealing that most of the children are employed illegally. Maybe they ought to be in day-care centers. Maybe they ought to be in school. But, from the time they can walk, there's work they can do. They can put potatoes in bushels. They can pull greens from the ground. Two-year-olds, three-year-olds, four-year-olds all work alongside their mothers.

One reporter, a modern muckraker, set out to discover just how government inspectors could be so fooled. This is the story he tells:

"The man put down his hamper. 'It sure looks like rain,' he said. The skies were a bright crystal blue, with only a trace of clouds to the east. The crew kept working, but a few looked up and saw three men coming down the row.

"One was the grower, who seldom came around. The other was the crew leader. The third man was a stranger. He carried a brown leather case and a clipboard. The men just nodded as they passed.

"They went up and down the rows, the first two walking easily. The third man, the stranger, stumbled now and then—a city man used to flat sidewalks.

"They crossed the red clay road and went into the south field. A woman looked up as they came past the stacks of empty crates. Before they were close enough to hear, she turned to the busy crew. 'Sure looks like rain.'

"Two small pickers dropped their boxes, darted through the vines, and ran into the woods. Someone on the next row passed the word. 'Sure looks like rain.' Two more children ducked into the vines and ran.

"The children hid beyond the road in a small clearing in a clump of scrub oaks. From here they could see the man leave. It was their favorite game. Hiding from the inspector was about the only thing that broke up the long hours in the field. In the camp, they played hide-and-seek this way. When you were 'it' you were the inspector."

As soon as the man with the clipboard left, the children returned in silence to bend over the vines they were plucking.

No wonder government inspectors can't tell whether one hundred thousand or six hundred thousand children are working as farm laborers.

Not only do these children work illegally for pennies a day, but they are always victims of disease. They almost never get to see a doctor. They don't receive the regular vaccinations all other children get to immunize them against smallpox, diphtheria, whooping cough, tetanus, polio.

Though they may be picking greens and berries, the migrant child laborers generally live on rice and corn. One report on a migrant camp in Texas showed that 96 per cent of the children had drunk no milk in six months. They suffer from diseases most people think have disappeared from the face of the earth. They have scurvy, rickets, protein deficiency.

In 1963, a migrant health bill was passed by the federal government. It provided money for individuals who would set up health programs for migrant workers. But the bill was written to last just two years. In 1965, it expired.

Just how much good could one law lasting two years do

Migrant children picking beans in Snowhill, Maryland

for those one hundred thousand or six hundred thousand starving children?

One doctor in Texas is so concerned about these children he can't pull himself and his practice away from the fields he hates to see.

"The children of migrant parents," he says, "are born into a world completely of their own. An anemic mother, and possibly a tubercular father—a life that will take him into his world where he may possibly die within one year, either from diarrhea, tuberculosis or malnutrition. His infancy would be a very close association with his brothers and sisters.

"Their home would be a one- or two-room shack with no inside running water and no flush toilets. If he lives to be of school age, he could possibly go to many schools on different occasions at different places, but will never average more than three years of schooling in his lifetime. His future life will be one of wandering, poverty and more sickness."

Fifty years after Camella Teoli told her dreadful story before a congressional committee, just a few years ago, a twelve-year-old girl working on a farm in Idaho got her hair caught in a potato-digging machine. Like the whirring mill wheels in Lawrence, the machine took the scalp with her hair. But this little girl was not so lucky as Camella. She didn't live to tell the tale. She died in the hospital several days after the accident.

Now, it is our turn to ask "Why?" Why is such horror permitted? What can we do to stop it?

Once again, the South speaks up to defend an indefensible position. Once again, we hear from North Carolina.

North Carolina's Congressman Cooley is the author of the Blue Sky Doctrine. "There are no sweatshops on the farms of America," according to Congressman Cooley. "On the farms of our nation, children labor with their parents under the blue skies."

When they should be in school?

When they should be sleeping and eating?

When they should be playing and growing?

They are just children, these migrant farm hands. And they cannot speak up for themselves. Yet, today, young people all over the world have begun to find their tongues. They are asking their governments to end wars. They are asking their schools to teach better. They are asking their families to know them better. They make sense. They speak well. But they are the children of affluence, these healthy, alert, energetic young people. They have enough education to be thinking of how schools should change and governments solve their problems.

Now, if they knew that in this land of plenty such pockets of poverty still exist, what would these affluent children do? Now that they've found their tongues?

Would they demand that laws be passed to end migrant child labor?

Would they help migrant children to speak out in their own cause?

Would they care?

INDEX